RIVER RUNTS

By Ted Merrill and Bill Merrill

Ted Merrill   *Bill Merrill*

3

Canadian Cataloguing in Publication Data

Merrill, Ted, 1923-
      River Runts / Ted Merrill & Bill Merrill; illustrations by
      Ted Merrill

ISBN 0-9731890-0-2

    1. Merrill, Ted, 1923- --Childhood and youth. 2. Merrill, Bill, 1924- --Childhood and youth. 3. Idaho–Description and travel. 4. Idaho–Biography. I. Merrill, Bill, 1924- II. Title

F752.A16M47 2002   979.6'032'0922   C2002-904958-X

First Printing - October 2002
Second Printing - May 2003

Printed by
Firgrove Publishing, Duncan, B.C.

Typesetting
Doris Benjamin

Graphics
Mailboxes Etc.

Illustrations
Ted Merrill

Printed by
FIRGROVE PUBLISHING
Duncan, B.C., Canada

The Authors

DEDICATION

To the memory of
Clifford D. Merrill and Esther Jacoby Merrill
who conceived us, nurtured us, and
set us free, we gratefully dedicate
this book

TABLE OF CONTENTS

SECTION ONE
Wood River Country and the Formative Years.

SECTION TWO
Salmon River and
The Marsh Creek Culture Hearth.

SECTION THREE
Back to Bigger Water and Bigger Deeds On Salmon River.

INTRODUCTION

We two brothers grew up together for some eighteen years – all the crucial years of self-creation, from embryo to fledgling to flying from the nest more or less intact and independent. As we have moved from telling our own children bedtime stories of "exciting adventures from my childhood," to jotting down a few recollections in our letters, to deciding to compile some fishing anecdotes, the process has become more and more a joint memoir of our adolescence and threatens to become a critique of parents, education, and society. Perhaps we have stopped in time.

We have written here exclusively of the summers of our youth, the out-of-school times for us and our school-teacher parents. They were spent in the Sawtooth Mountains of central Idaho, some hundred and twenty miles from our home in Fairfield. Through the retrospectoscope they appear as isolated vignettes of treasured places and events, but focussing more clearly we can see also an orderly progression of lessons learned and skills gained, of culture and values being passed on – and the passing of an era on our planet.

From two to three months each summer was spent in the mountains, camping or, in some years, living in a cabin or an old house on the river. After three summers in Ketchum we camped for four summers along the Wood River; then Dad began hearing more and more stories of the salmon that were being taken in the upper Salmon River and its tributaries, and we began spending our summers there.

The time and geography divide themselves into three parts: the Wood River years of nurture; the orientation years on Salmon River and then on Marsh Creek; and then moving back to bigger water and bigger deeds on Salmon River again.

In comparing our growing up with that of our own children we have noted that, whatever we or they feel they have missed, the world has changed greatly even in this short span of years, a mere half a lifetime, and the environment in which we had our origins no longer exists. We offer that concern as counterpoint to these stories of the finest of times.

SECTION ONE

Wood River Country and the Formative Years

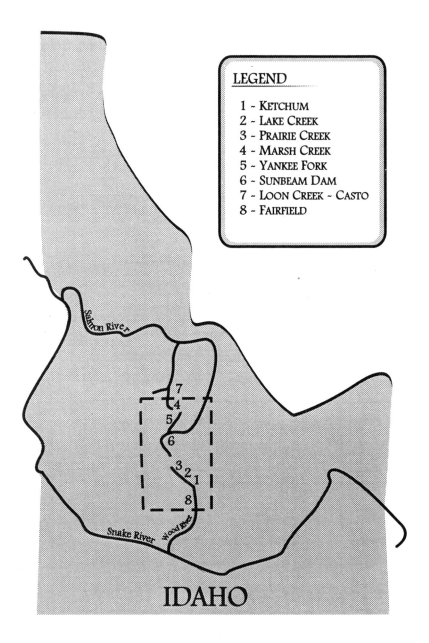

LEGEND

1 ~ KETCHUM
2 ~ LAKE CREEK
3 ~ PRAIRIE CREEK
4 ~ MARSH CREEK
5 ~ YANKEE FORK
6 ~ SUNBEAM DAM
7 ~ LOON CREEK ~ CASTO
8 ~ FAIRFIELD

Salmon River

Snake River   Wood River

IDAHO

DAD LEARNS TO FISH

Some fishermen are made, not born. When I was four years old our father was utterly scornful of fishing as a great waste of time, and my only fishing experience had been sitting with my uncle in a boat in a small, muddy pond, trying to understand the rationale of impaling a small fish on a hook and then dangling it in the water in the hope of somehow attracting another (presumably larger) fish.

The summer that I was five, we stayed in Ketchum, Idaho. Ketchum, next to the now famous Sun Valley, was then a quiet little town at the end of the railroad, noted mainly for annually shipping out the large numbers of sheep raised along Wood River.

Our mother ran the dining room in the old, log cabin-style, two-story Ketchum Kamp Hotel.

Dad, who was a school teacher the rest of the year, ran a "taxi" service, twice a week carrying passengers and bringing back fresh vegetables for the hotel via a two-hundred-mile loop, on a largely one-track road, over Trail Creek Summit to Carey and Arco, then across to Challis on the Salmon River, up past Sunbeam Dam and Stanley to Galena Summit (which gives rise to the headwaters of the Salmon River on one side of the hill and Wood River on the other side) and thence home to Ketchum. My brother Billy and I occupied ourselves in assorted ways and got under foot.

Many of the hotel guests were fishermen. Some came from far away and spent time, money, and eager effort on catching trout. Dad, being a perceptive man, began to wonder whether there might be aspects of fishing that he had missed; there must be something to it, or there wouldn't be so many grown up and apparently sensible people so excited about it.

He decided to find out, once and for all. He asked two of the guests if he might go along and watch them fish. They offered to provide him with tackle, but he declined.

After two days of watching these fly fishermen, Dad went to the hardware store and bought a telescoping steel rod, a twenty-five-cent reel, an enameled silk line, three or four flies, and gut leader. Then he went out alone, firmly rejecting any offers of company, help, or advice. For two days, from after lunch until dark, he was gone but brought back no fish. The next day he caught two small trout; the next day six or seven.

By the end of that summer Dad was a confirmed and accomplished fisherman. By then he was willing to learn from others, and two of his school-teaching colleagues gave him useful pointers. Within two more years he had invested in more sophisticated equipment – a split bamboo fly rod, tapered fly line, and automatic reel – and a few of his flies were olive quills imported from England. I remember standing by the tent and watching, marvelling at the grace and fluidity and complete control of the movement as his line was lifted from the water, the long sinuous flow of the back-cast high over the tules and sage brush bordering Silver Creek, and the sun-gilded line moving smoothly back over the stream to drop the fly flawlessly again upon the water. In my memory and perception of him, Silver Creek was a central part of Dad's being. He would leave camp at sunup "to fish a while before breakfast," and return at one or two in the afternoon, his creel filled with huge rainbow trout. At Silver Creek he usually released any fish under three pounds. Meanwhile Mom bit her lip and envisioned him drowned somewhere in the quicksand, or hopelessly tried to arrange meals to fit everybody's needs.

At this point Bill and I were too young to fish with him except in rather special situations, but I deeply sensed the integrity and purity of what he was doing, the romance – almost religion – that united the devoted and sufficiently skilled initiate with that mystical world beneath the surface of almost any body of water. He had found out what fishing was all about, and it became for him both an art medium and a means of expressing and communicating to his children and his associates much of his character, his value system, and his world view.

FIRSTS

Bill is nineteen months and one day younger than I am. Now, when we're both in our third quarter-century, that is the least of the differences between us, but in the first few years of life it's a big gap. For a long time, through cosmic accident of birth order, I was bigger, more capable, hence had many opportunities to savor new life experiences before he did: I was first to be born, first to watch the cow being milked, first to see kittens being born, and countless other firsts that are lost to memory.

But Bill was first to catch a fish. Dad was going fishing with some friend or relative in Clear Lake, in the Snake River canyon near Twin Falls – going fishing in a boat, something he did rarely and never with enthusiasm. However, go in a boat he did, and both Bill and I, ages four-and-a-half and six, were to be taken along. As fate decreed, I was sick on the appointed day, and had to stay miserably at home.

When the fishermen returned in the afternoon, Bill had caught a fish! The fact that it was taken by trolling, and with a bit of assistance here and there, so that no high degree of technical skill was required, certainly took nothing away from the honor of catching a good keeping-sized trout at his tender age; I was appropriately pleased and proud of him. Privately I consoled myself with the thought that, given similar circumstances, I would probably have performed as valiantly, and that, after all, there were few enough chances he got to outdo me.

It was quite a while later before I caught my first fish. I well remember putting in the apprenticeship, with the most rudimentary equipment – a willow stick with a piece of string attached, and one of our mother's hairpins tied on the end – standing on a stone a full two feet out in the edge of a shallow riffle on Wood River, practicing casting. (They thought I was playing, pretending to fish; but I was dead serious, and practicing. And after all, maybe even a fish could make a mistake and think the hairpin was something else.)

After a time a fisherman came along, a stranger wading jauntily down the stream in high rubber waders and carrying a fine-looking rod – a lot like Dad's. He greeted me, and inquired how I was doing and what I was fishing with. I tried to retain some dignity as I explained to him that I didn't really expect to catch anything on a hairpin, but was just practicing.

"Hm!" he said. "Maybe this would work better." And he tied onto the end of my string a big red fly, a real artificial fly tied on a real hook, bigger than any of Dad's that I had ever seen and quite the most glorious fly in the world! I stammered my thanks; he wished me luck, and disappeared around the bend.

Now I was no longer just practicing, I was fishing! I knew that casting a fly a mere four feet from my hand in four inches of water was not the ideal approach, but that was merely a matter of adjusting the odds. This was for real!

I kept up the casting until it was nearly too dark to see the water, while Mom stepped over more and more often to see whether I wasn't getting tired of it and ready to quit.

Finally the inevitable happened: a clumsy cast imbedded the fly securely in the front of my sweater. I couldn't get it out, and so adjourned the few yards back to camp to show Mom my prize and my problem.

She was impressed by the fly; was not surprised, I believe, that it was caught in the sweater; and elected to wait for Dad to extricate it.

It wasn't long (full dark now) until he returned, and I proudly displayed the fly. Though he made appropriate sounds, I sensed that he was a bit put out that I had my first fly from a stranger instead of from him; or maybe it wasn't the fly he would have selected. At any rate he perceived the problem of the hook in the sweater and agreed to take care of it. He took out his pocket knife and carefully cut the fly from the end of the string. I thought, "I hope he doesn't have to cut too big a hole in the sweater," and watched him approach with the knife once more. Suddenly I was filled with horror as, with one deft sweep, he stripped the red feathers and thread, wings, hackle and all, from the shank of the hook, leaving a naked, obscenely shiny piece of empty metal – which he then easily pushed on through to remove it from the sweater.

I was paralyzed, speechless. It was too late to protest. I tried to murmur, "I thought you were going to cut the sweater," but I couldn't hear how it came out. I could hardly believe what had happened.

Finally Dad realized that there were tears in my eyes, and he gently pointed out that a sweater costs more than a fly. "Don't worry," he said, "we'll get you another fly."

(Oh, fine! Never mind that your child has just been eaten by sharks; we'll get you another.)

I realized, eventually, that it was just a matter of a different point of view, and that Dad couldn't really have known how I felt about the fly. But the event always represented to me one of Dad's rare lapses of sensitivity – and I wonder now, as a parent, how often I have done the same sort of thing, failing to read my child's mind.

It may have been later that summer, or the next (I recall feeling noticeably more mature) when I was provided with a real fishing outfit – having "earned" it by showing sufficient interest and dedication to fishing. It was a telescoping steel rod such as Dad, Bill, and I all used as beginners. I was taken along with Dad and a friend (I can't remember who it was now – doubtless I'm subconsciously repressing the memory), and was left fishing at one hole while

Dad moved around a small clump of willows to the next one. He had pointed out to me that in this spot a small eddy would keep my fly moving around and around in a good place if I would cast it out there (about eight feet).

After twenty minutes or so our friend came by, and stopped to inquire whether I had caught any.

"Not yet," I replied.

"Looks like you may have something on there," he said.

I lifted the rod a bit, and was astonished – and humiliated – to realize that there was a seven-inch trout hanging open-mouthed and long since drowned and dead on my hook; it didn't oblige with so much as a quiver as I sheepishly lifted it out onto the bank.

Oh, well, you have to start someplace.

It was not many years until the age difference between me and Bill began melting away. Our parents always made every effort to be fair, and often arranged to compensate in some way when one of us had an opportunity or stroke of fortune that the other didn't. They generally encouraged us – often at the cost of some anxiety, I'm sure – to be independent and to keep expanding our repertoire of skill, while being as careful as possible to assure our safety. I don't know at what age Bill became my equal as a fisherman and outdoorsman, but it happened somewhere along there when we weren't looking. When one summer the folks had to go home for business and, with some trepidation, left Bill and me, ages perhaps sixteen and eighteen, at Sunbeam for a few weeks by ourselves, we functioned as a comfortably co-equal team of salmon fishing guides.

SUMMERS OF OUR GREAT CONTENT

Lake Creek is really the name of a lake; or actually, a place; more properly, even, of an era. It was at Lake Creek, near Wood River, a few miles above Ketchum, that we first spent a whole summer – two months or so – camping, living from a tent and car. Two summers we were there, when I was seven and eight, and the two are fused in my mind with no interruptions between them – except for the rabbits. During one of the summers Papa and Nanan, Dad's parents, camped with us.

One might wonder why our folks chose this place -- rather barren, as campgrounds go, a little basin in which gravel, sagebrush, and a bit of grass and weeds slope gently down to the edge of a small lake. On the other side a tree-covered hill came down almost to the edge of the water, but on our side there were no trees. The six-by-six pyramid tent was staked out on a small grassy spot, to serve as dressing room, storage room, bedroom for Mom and Dad, and general retreat in bad weather. A canvas tarp was tied to the car and extended out to the tops of saplings guyed with ropes and stakes, to form a canopy over the table. Bill and I slept in the car. Papa and Nanan had their car and tent just behind ours.

The lake itself was actually a large beaver pond. The dam, built of logs and sticks and plastered with mud in typical beaver fashion, was about forty feet long, and created a pond perhaps two hundred feet wide and six hundred feet long (dimensions, seen through the prisms of child's vision and elapsed years, are highly negotiable) and shaped like an hour-glass. One could walk across the top of the dam, which lay a good long cast from the cooking fire, and easily get to the other side of the lake. There was no place where the bank dropped abruptly into deep water – maybe one of the reasons for choosing this place to camp with small children. The rules were clear: never go out of direct line-of-sight from camp, and never wade into water to a depth above the knees without permission and direct supervision. Our knees were very close to the ground in those days, so that even on the shallow side near the dam the rule didn't permit us far enough out from shore to be much help for fishing. Standing on my favorite rock, a chunk of feldspar the size of a foot locker that just dipped its toes in the water, I got at least psychological if not mechanical advantage from the extra eighteen inches of altitude while trying to cast.

This was the place where I learned fly casting -- and learned, and learned. (I am eternally thankful that I came along before the advent of spinning gear, or I might never have learned to cast a fly.) The equipment was crude, for fly casting: a six-foot telescoping steel rod, a reel not much bigger than a pocket watch, and an enameled silk line that tended to retain the shape of the reel as it unwound. It was the same rig, in fact, that Dad had used in learning to fish some three or four years earlier.

On this rock I internalized the seventeenth century dictum of Charles Cotton that I came upon decades later: "fish fine and far away." There was scarce a time when you could look out over the lake and not see somewhere the concentric ripples marking a rising trout; but they were invariably "far away" beyond the reach of my flailing cast, and my presentation was rarely "fine." If I got off a zinging thirty-foot offering I was happy but the fish were unimpressed. I learned (at the cost of a good many of Dad's patiently provided flies) how to avoid whip-cracking the leader on the back-cast and snapping the fly off. I learned (more or less) how to keep my back-cast up out of the weeds and off of the mullein stalks (walk back and break down the mullein stalks) and how to cope with a head wind (go on the other side of the lake). I learned patience, and the pleasant art of meditating and doing nothing at all for hours at a time while appearing to be constantly casting a fly.

My present preference (a far from exclusive or purist choice) for fishing with flies stems no doubt from the fact that Dad's fishing had started this way, and from the further fact that for a beginner it's much easier. Dad could fix me up with a fly and then go off and fish the morning, whereas if I were using bait there would have been endless problems; after a series of false casts, drooping back-casts, and collapsing coils out front, the fly is likely to be still there, while a salmon egg or even a worm would long since have been thrashed away before ever approaching fish country. Casting bait in a small clear lake with fly tackle requires a delicate touch. Thus for better or worse I fished with flies, and loved it.

I suppose that during that first summer, fishing two to several hours daily, I may have caught five fish, and the second summer perhaps twenty. I remember only one time when in a single session I scored repeatedly. I was casting from the far shore, with evening shadows closing in and a stiff breeze at my back, when it began to rain gently. I was about to call it quits – partly because I could no longer see my fly nor make it float – when I felt that sudden adrenalin rush of a fish on the line, and in a few moments held in my trembling hands a nine-inch, gorgeously colored "brookie." Accustomed to thinking of such happy events as accidents, I nevertheless resumed my efforts, casting onto the dark surface of the water now shredded by wind and pelting rain. I could let the wind do most of the job of casting, the line flapping up and down like a flag until I forced it down onto the water with my rod tip and retrieved it in short pulls. In a few minutes I caught another fish. Mom shouted across to me the obvious fact that it was raining, but I waved my two trout and continued casting. After the fourth fish the rain ceased, and so did the action. As darkness fell I finally adjourned, drenched, shivering, and ecstatic.

The second summer we brought rabbits. During the school year, starting with a male and two female chinchilla bunnies, Bill and I were rapidly initiated into the ways of rabbits, including their remarkable enthusiasm and proficiency at breeding, eating, and excreting. Dad kept building more pens; Bill and I kept ranging farther afield in the surrounding vacant lots and roadsides to cut grass and alfalfa, feeding hay in winter and seeking more efficient ways of cleaning the cages.

By summer, when we went camping, despite having eaten rabbit meat all winter, we gave away forty-eight rabbits and took the last ten young ones in a portable cage to Lake Creek. Here the technique was simple: we merely added water, and moved the pen twice a day to a new grassy spot so the black pellets were left behind and the next meal protruded up through the wire mesh. We ate the poor things soon enough to eliminate the danger of proliferation.

At Lake Creek I first became acquainted with cicadas, and to hear their harsh grating song in the trees even now takes me back nostalgically to the water's edge at the narrow waist of the lake where Dad first explained, and showed me, the source of the sound. The cicada is a wondrous creature which, after burrowing into the ground as an infantile nymph, stays seventeen years under the hard soil to mature into adult form! It is also a heavy, meaty insect and a trout's delight. Dad demonstrated this by casting one, impaled on his fly, out onto the breast of the lake, where it was instantly smitten by a fish.

The eagerness with which cicadas were hailed as bait was tempered by the difficulty of keeping one on the hook long enough to get it out to the fish. Dad's response to this problem was to create an artificial cicada. He was just getting into fly tying, and his lack of experience and finesse was made up for by his ingenuity. His first cicada was strikingly lifelike, with a thick black body built up with electrician's tape, wings made of cellophane from a package of Lucky Strikes, and enough orange thread wound here and there to complete the overall cicada effect. He stepped to the edge of the lake and made his first cast; the fly shot out over the water, landed with a mighty splash, and sank like a stone to the bottom.

Back to the drawing board. This time he built a body from a piece of cork. There were difficulties in getting it to stay on the hook, and it seemed rather rickety and disheveled compared to the first one, but it gave the general idea of a cicada. In those ancient pre-nylon days, fishing leaders were made of catgut (actually, the muscle layer of a sheep's intestine) and had to be soaked thoroughly before tying a knot, otherwise they were stiff and brittle. But anticipatory tension was mounting in the cicada venture; Dad gave his leader a couple of quick impatient licks, then tied on the object. My brother and I hovered breathlessly nearby as he once more offered his creation to the fish. This time it floated out through the air and dropped light as a feather on the water. A few seconds passed, there was the swirl of a fish, Dad raised his rod sharply to set the hook, and the leader parted. The entire action was over so quickly that we all stood in stunned silence. Dad let his line lie motionless in the water, then slowly took out his fly box to select a ginger quill. Thus ended any but esthetic concern with the cicada.

Bill and I played in the little stream that flowed out of the lake through the sieve-like fabric of the beaver dam. It twinkled down among moss-covered rocks, past the spring where Dad had rigged a wooden spout for filling buckets with bitingly cold drinking water, and thence it plunged into a dark and enticing channel under willows and vines which, being out of sight of camp, was generally forbidden to us. We decided to try the beavers' game and dam off a little side diversion of the creek to make a private and fish-tight pool. There has always been for me some compellingly mystical attraction to building a little pond that could enclose – if I had one – a fish.

This is a nifty engineering problem: to let water in and out through barriers sufficiently stable but with no orifices large enough to let a fish out, and not let the water go over the top either, while using only the materials at hand. (I don't believe beavers concern themselves with fugitive fish.) After days of trial and error, using rocks, sticks, gravel, and sand, we finally achieved it, having lost two trout in the testing. Since almost any place where a fish might be caught (mostly by Dad) was only a quick sprint from our aquatic stockade, we managed at one time to have five or six fish in store, to impress visitors or (after we became inured to the idea) to supplement a short skilletful. Once a guest was almost reduced to tears when he learned that, having accidentally lost two fish from his catch into the stream while cleaning them for him, I had replaced them with two of our "pets."

I have never understood the biology of a place like Lake Creek, where all the fish are the same size. The lake was teeming with Eastern Brook trout – the only kind I ever saw caught there – and invariably their size was between eight and ten inches; I'm sure that one could often lay out ten consecutive "brookies" and find less than an inch of difference among their lengths. (I refuse to believe that these were hatchery fish.) However, the year before our Lake Creek summer, a friend of Dad's woke him at about two in the morning to show him a twenty-four inch Eastern Brook he had caught in the dark at Lake Creek. As we sour-grapes anglers are wont to say, it must have been the only one out there.

Exactly fifty years later I returned to Lake Creek, bent on showing my second wife the places of my childhood nurture, the cradle of my being.

People had warned me. "You won't recognize it," they said. "It's changed so much, all built up." With trepidation I drove from Hailey up Wood River toward Ketchum, and found myself almost regretting having come. Just as they had said, the original spare, faintly-populated area with an occasional old log house or crumbling remains of a settlement, nestled between the rows of hills or mountains on either side of the valley, was now defaced by the wounds of recent construction; rich folks' houses, condominiums, bed-and-breakfast, and white-washed fences were scattered along the river; the road had been widened and paved; there were even a few mailboxes on posts by the road.

Ketchum, in those olden times before Averill Harriman turned his attention from the Union Pacific Railroad long enough to build Sun Valley, was a little mountain village, and a sheep-shipping town. More lambs were shipped out of Ketchum each year than from any other place in the world. Now, a half-century later, the former sheep pens were gone but the wide dusty flat down by the river where they had been was still recognizable from the highway.

As we moved on upriver from Ketchum it got worse. The road was lined with houses, cars, and people. Driving slowly, I scanned the road-side for the sign. It was right where it was supposed to be, two miles from town, a little board nailed to a post: "Lake Creek." We turned off on a narrow blacktop road between a pair of what I considered overly ostentatious homes, past a small housing development, and my heart sank. But we were this close, I had to see it through. We rounded a bend in the road and approached a barbed wire fence bearing a sign, "Entering U. S. Forest Service Property."

I could hardly believe my eyes. There was nothing beyond the fence but sagebrush. The asphalt ended, and we were on a narrow one-track dirt road winding among the low hills, exactly as I remembered it. I recalled that about a mile ahead had been an old cottonwood tree where a sheepherder camped with his wagon, canvas-covered like a small version of the old Conestogas, while his flock nibbled their way along the hillsides beyond. It was along here that my father had first showed me his favorite flower, the sego lily, which grew profusely here (profuse, for the sego lily, means a flower every thirty feet or so).

A few bends and curves farther along, a dust cloud trailing in our wake, I stopped abruptly. A few hundred yards off to the right was a battered pickup truck. In a chair, under a tree, a man was reading. And the bed of the pickup was covered with canvas stretched over bows just like on the old covered wagons, though smaller. I couldn't see the sheep, but this was unmistakably a sheepherder! I drove on, heart pounding. As we reached the final bend in the road two people on horses were riding away, back the way we had come, and there was the lake.

This was a bizarre, almost frightening feeling, like entering an improbable dream. The lake, the beaver dam, the hill thrown across the upper end of the basin, the gurgling creek below the dam – it was all there, each part checked against the indelible print in my memory and finding a perfect fit.

We got out of the car and walked around slowly.

"Right by this granite boulder," I said, "was the cooking stove. The trough for the spring water is gone."

The dam appeared a bit shorter, and there were a few faint marks from bulldozer treads at its near end; someone (not beaver) had done some limited repair. I walked along the shore toward the north, and carefully stepped up onto the

25

chunk of feldspar at the water's edge. From here, by angling my head just right I could see three small brook trout lying motionless below the surface. Far across the pond was a ring of ripples left by a feeding trout.

We returned to the car. A half hour was enough; I dared not risk staying longer.

There's a saying, "You can't step in the same river twice." Maybe so. But I'm here to say that, by some sleight of mind or warp of time, I have very nearly stepped twice in that same river.

PRAIRIE CREEK

Prairie Creek flowed, and perhaps still flows, into the Big Wood River a few miles above Ketchum. There was a Forest Service Ranger Station nearby. I remember clean white buildings with green roofs, a flag pole, and the only patches of green lawn we would see all summer. Memories of that summer are vignettes, bits of people, bits of stream, big black and white dog, bits of seven-year-old encounters. That summer created its share of family lore, confusing memory with later story telling but not clouding the sharpest images.

It was the summer of 1932, and holds the first recollections I have of fishing with my brother Ted independently of our father. The terms set for this stunning degree of freedom and their implementation have in retrospect told me volumes about our parents and their views of parenting. Our unaccompanied ventures along Wood River were subject to two and only two rules: we could fish where we liked as long as 1) we stayed constantly within sight of each other, and 2) we always told the folks whether we were going upstream or downstream.

We clearly understood the logic of these rules. Their absolute nature was impressed upon us one day when we returned to camp from the wrong direction. We had, with due notice, set out upstream. After an hour or so, the river being suddenly devoid of fish, we passed the camp and fished downstream. Since the folks were napping, we decided not to disturb them. It was a mistake in judgement, a failure properly to order priorities, which we did not make again. As I recall, we were asked to consider the relative importance to our parents of being awakened from a nap, or vainly searching for us in the wrong direction.

Our camp near the junction of Prairie Creek and Wood River was in an open stand of lodgepole pines. Across the river were occasional wide grassy meadows in which sage grouse dwelt. Young sage grouse, properly dressed and cooked as our mother cooked them is a gourmet delight rarely equalled. So our father would from time to time venture against them, armed with a .410-gauge pistol. A meagre weapon, to be sure. The only birds likely to fall prey to such a gun are undisturbed sage grouse and caged canaries. The former, however, have such a myopic view of life and such lousy judgement about when to fly that they quite often graced our table.

Mythology has it (and probably rightly so) that the sage grouse, in order to be edible, must be field stripped the moment it is killed. This field stripping, as taught to us by our father, goes like this: After making sure that the fallen bird is dead, one takes the tail feathers in the left hand close to the body, and inserts the right forefinger in the bird's anus. A quick rip, and the viscera can be slung out onto the ground with a minimum of fuss. (This prevents the sage leaves in the bird's digestive tract from over-spicing the flesh before it is cooked.) And thereby hangs a tale:

A teaching colleague of our father's, a rather dainty and fastidious man, came to spend a few days with us at our Prairie Creek camp. While there he expressed the desire to hunt sage grouse, the ideal beginner's game. Dad carefully instructed him in the use of the pistol and in the care of the game. (Fixed ritual in our family required that the one who killed game cared for it afterward, and no exceptions could be allowed for guests.)

We set off through the tall grass of a nearby meadow, Dad and Ted and I in a row as beaters, with our guest in the center of the line. A flock got up at our feet, our guest fired, a bird fell. He raced after it and picked it up. There was nothing for it, so he upended it and with infinite distaste inserted his forefinger, crooked it, and prepared to rip. The bird flew away.

Now this was no ordinary sage grouse. No succulent young dinner, it was a veritable Ulysses of its race. It was huge and grey and old, a sire of sires. It had a two-inch beak and three-inch spurs, and wing joints like hickory cudgels. Hooked on our hapless guest's forefinger, it led him at a dead run across the meadow. He would pull the bird to him, get beaten and spurred, and allow the bird to carry him on. Collapsed in laughter, we couldn't have helped if we would. My memory goes no further. Our guest runs off the edge of the years, the great grouse leading him by his arm, while we gasp and cry in the sweet grass.

LEAVE NO STONE UNRETURNED

At Prairie Creek Dad introduced us to periwinkles, and to rock-turning ethic.

I see him standing in the shallow water at the edge of Wood River, reaching down to bring up a rock the size of his head and turn it over. There on the underside of the rock was a black, scary, lizard-like, flat creature an inch and a half long which immediately scampered to the edge of the rock and dropped back into the water. A hellgrammite, Dad said, and good bait, too; but what we were concerned with this time were the five or six other objects projecting at an angle from the rock. They looked like little fingers made of sand, about an inch long and almost as thick as a pencil, attached firmly to the rock at one end. Dad pulled one off and broke it in two; it turned out to be a hollow shell, and inside was a a yellow grub-like larva, tough and firm, with a black head and short black legs. This, we were told, would be very exciting to any trout who saw it, and the rest of the little shell cases were carefully collected and dropped into the fish sack.

Dad then stepped back out into the water and put the stone, bottom side down, back in about the same place where he found it. The reason, he pointed out, was that the stone and the space under it had been the home of a variety of creatures (indeed we had seen the hellgrammite, and a number of tiny slithery things, and some unidentified dark little blobs and bits of jelly-like stuff on the rock, in addition to the periwinkles). It is better, he said, to take only enough periwinkles for the immediate fishing needs, and to turn the stones back over into their original spots so the communities that live there can find their places again, and so that there will be periwinkles and hellgrammites when we want them in the future.

This was part of the intuitive ecological sensitivity (though I'm not sure he even knew the word "ecology") that typified Dad's living and his relationships with people and other creatures.

We later learned that the hellgrammite is the carnivorous pupal stage of the salmon or stone fly (which itself is good bait), and that the periwinkle (local usage for a word that is more widely applied to very different creatures) is the caddisworm, larva of the caddis fly. There are many species of these, varying in size from our sandy friends on down; they spin their little houses from silk, and then glue up the outsides with sand, wood splinters, pine needles, bits of shell, etc., depending on the species and on what is available. If you find the periwinkle a bit later in its development the tough cylindrical worm has turned into a soft, squishy, pinkish orange, partly translucent pupa, the embryonic insect, with long legs, folded wings, and antennae. Though we convinced ourselves that the fish like this stage better, it's not as good for fishing because it's too soft to stay on the hook. But it's worth finding just as a reminder that the plain stubby little worm does indeed turn into a complex and more graceful creature of the airways.

SECTION TWO

Salmon River
and
The Marsh Creek
Culture Hearth

ON THE SALMON

I suppose it was in 1929 that I first saw a chinook salmon. My first memory of these incredible fish was the sight of them jumping at the spillway tunnel of the old Sunbeam Dam. A great gout of water roared out of an eight-foot diameter rock tunnel, under such a head of pressure that it was mid-summer before the river eased up enough for the fish to negotiate it. But every year some did, so that they could spawn upriver and their progeny would be back, jumping and resting to jump again. Huge fish, black against the white water. Few images from childhood remain as sharp as those.

The chinook salmon and the great whales somehow occupy a similar niche in my cosmology of natural wonders and human follies. They are the largest of their respective kinds. They are deeply imbedded in the history and folklore of peoples who have been their respective neighbors. On the British Columbia coast they both were integral parts of the lives of the same peoples. They share an incomplete attachment to the ocean, the salmon entering fresh water to spawn and die, and the whale entering the atmosphere every hour or so for oxygen. Both have been reverently and gratefully preyed upon by men for thousands of years. (I have killed hundreds of chinook salmon. Discovering, long after, the Salish purification ritual, assuring that the hunter is physically and spiritually worthy of the hunted, leaves me with a twinge of doubt.) Both have been savagely, ungratefully and irreverently preyed upon by men of Western-European-North American culture armed with industrial weapons for about a century and a half. And unless we moderns are overtaken by a cataclysmic wave of sanity, both are probably doomed.

But here the similarity ceases. The great whales have been the direct victims of modern warfare, waged with increasingly sophisticated weapons. They were mined, first for light and lubricants, then for dog food. The salmon have met this; but more, their rivers have been blocked, fouled and heated until the remaining fresh-water habitat is a miserable tithe of what is needed. At least the whales have fallen to a direct foe. The salmon have been destroyed by heedlessness, by a callous and casual carelessness unthinkable to more reasonable stewards of life's largess.

The Great Depression of the 1930s probably fell more heavily on the chinook salmon than on any other living thing, including man. The wave of public works brought the U. S. Corps of Engineers and the Bureau of Reclamation into every major watershed in the western United States, including those used by the Pacific salmon. The mission of the one was to pour concrete, and of the other to increase the acreage of agricultural land. To both, the salmon constituted a public relations problem which will end when the salmon are gone.

SALMON AND SPAWNING

Salmon are anadromous fish; that is, they are hatched in fresh water, swim downstream to the sea and grow up in salt water. When it is time to reproduce – usually after two to four years – they swim back upstream to spawn, returning unerringly to the same stream where they were born.

The various Pacific salmon (genus Oncorhynchus) – unlike steelhead trout and Atlantic salmon (genus Salmo)[1] – never eat again from the time they leave the ocean; they make the trip, do their spawning, and then die. By the time the chinook[2] reaches the upper Salmon River – a trip of some 900 to 1,000 miles, including some pretty rough terrain – its digestive tract is empty and atrophied, the fish has lost up to a third of its original weight, and its abdominal cavity contains hardly anything except the rather large liver and the spawn. In the male this consists of two long, white, spongy cigar shaped testes full of milky fluid (a suspension of the sperm cells); in the female, up to two quarts of translucent orange-red eggs

---

[1]

In our time this was the official nomenclature. In recent years some presumptuous taxonomists, on grounds of anatomical similarities, have changed the genealogy. Now steelhead trout, rainbow trout, and cutthroat trout have joined the various species of Pacific salmon in the genus *Oncorhynchus*, while the brown trout and the Atlantic salmon are still *Salmo*. Although these experts, of course, have the final say, we accept this only reluctantly because the old designation so neatly separated the spawn-once-and-die fish from the spawn-and-live-to-spawn-again types. Take your choice.

[2]

Known elsewhere also as spring, king, tyee, smiley, etc. Of the several species of Pacific salmon, only the chinook and the sockeye reach the Salmon River.

The fish undergo a great physiologic change before spawning, becoming weak and flabby, with pale flesh, very poor for food, with their biological tide ebbing fast; but this change takes place mainly in the last two or three weeks of life. Despite the rigorous journey, the long fast and the weight loss, the fish arriving at Sunbeam Dam in June and July are still several weeks from spawning and are strong, vigorous fish, formidable contestants on the end of a line and delectable at the table.

I suppose the salmon family structuring could be called matriarchal. The female, arriving at the spawning stream of her foremothers and of her own birth, selects a shallow gravelly riffle perhaps three or four feet deep. Her days of nourishing her own flesh being past, she has apparently only two activities to vie for her time: resting, and depositing her eggs beneath a shallow layer of sand and gravel. First using her tail as a shovel or broom, she begins to scrape out the bed, a depression several inches deep, four to six feet wide, and ten to twenty feet long. (These are deeper than they look; more than once I have thought I could wade across the center of such a bed, and nearly got my shirt pockets wet.)

Once the spot is selected and the bed started, the female generally will stay there until she finishes spawning and dies. It is an intriguing sight to see a big fish turn partly on her side and waggle back and forth so that her underside pushes the gravel off to the side and sends a cloud of silt and sand drifting downstream.

A few seconds of this at a time, repeated every couple of minutes with occasional longer breaks, over two or three days, is enough to produce the easily visible light-colored area where the sediment and algae-covered pebbles have been replaced with the freshly exposed lighter-colored surfaces of a deeper layer.

When she has things well established, the males begin to show up and lay claim to family rights (conjugal would hardly be the right term, given the technique of the salmon). The female, ignoring the males completely, will enter the lower end of the bed and repeat the gravel-stirring maneuver but now also releasing eggs at the same time so that at least some of them end up covered by a fine layer of sand.

The male, who has been hovering and waiting just downstream, moves up three or four feet behind her and repeats a reduced version of the same maneuver, releasing little milky-looking puffs or clouds of sperm near where the eggs have just been deposited; these tiny carriers of destiny enter the long-shot gamble of drifting downstream on the chance that an occasional one here and there will float through the gravel hiding place and make effective contact with an egg. With sufficient millions of possibilities, some do achieve this improbable connection and make the whole amazing journey worth-while.

The female continues these activities off and on for a week or more. During this time, a constant parade of males may come and go, though often a single male, by dint of superior size, physical prowess, determination, or persistence (I suppose) takes over and others may appear only fleetingly. Since the fish that have already started to spawn have also begun to lose the fine flavor and pink-orange color of their flesh and much of their vigor, and since we always felt a twinge of conscience at taking a fish that was just about to consummate the final stage and goal of its life's effort, we seldom took a fish from a spawning bed. However, it was known to be possible to take a "fresh" male from the spot every morning for a week, and the female would continue her business in steadfast and single-minded efficiency; but take away the female, and the bed would be deserted for the rest of the season.

During their long trek from the sea without food these fish show remarkably little change except for the loss of weight; in the last miles they fight hard in the catching, taste good in the eating, and are relatively unscarred from negotiating all the thousand miles or so of hazards, and up until mid-July sometimes still carry on their fins or bellies the "sea lice", or small leeches that have ridden with them from salt water. But once the actual spot is reached and spawning started, an amazingly rapid change takes place. I don't know in terms of physiology or pathology just what makes the difference, but within the two or three week period of spawning and after, the fish becomes weak and listless, and will struggle very little if hooked. It develops white, shaggy patches on the head, back, and fins; the fins are worn and shredded from the digging in the gravel; the belly, now empty of spawn, is hollow and gaunt. Both male and female tend to hang around the area of the spawning bed for a few more days, becoming visibly weaker day by day. Like the storied portrait of Dorian Gray, the fish change almost over night from the prime of life to senescence and death. Finally it is too much even to struggle against the gentle current, and the fish turns on its side, rolls slowly over and over, and is carried away out of sight into the deeper water below.

Romantic myth has it that the parent is still carrying out its "purpose" by providing the young with food after they have hatched and started downstream. So far as I can determine, this probably does not happen in a literal and direct sense; yet indirectly it obviously does. The fish has carried in its body a load of protein from the ocean to the spawning spot, thus newly enriching the nutrient load of the stream. Through courtesy of our invisible little friends, the bacteria and fungi which clean up after the party of living, the bodies of the fish are liberated and inserted back into the very bottom of the food chain, to be recycled back around the chemical carousel of life as are we all.

TOOLS OF THE TRADE

Salmon River begins just on the north side of Galena Summit, after you leave the Wood River valley at its upper end. From here, where the mighty Salmon runs through a culvert under the road and is hardly enough to wet your ankles, you can look to the north and see several miles of the meandering, rapidly growing stream, and can just about see where Pole Creek comes in from the east. From Pole Creek on down about forty miles to Clayton, the Salmon River was to become our family's fishing domain, principal vacation area, and workshop for growing up, through the years from 1933 until around 1943 when Bill and I both had reached almost full size and had gone off to college or the Navy.

As our familiarity with the river grew, the commonly known and named landmarks became insufficient for our purposes, and gradually a series of names evolved for notable fishing holes: the Mouth of Redfish Lake Creek; the Cliff Hole; the Pot Hole; the Bauscher Hole (named for friends who caught a fish there); the Snag Hole; the Basin Creek Hole; the House Rock; the American Creek Hole; the Harden Creek Hole; the Hot Springs (hot sulphur spring, with a little building for bathing and laundry); the Dam; the Mouth of Yankee Fork; the cliff below Yankee Fork; the Big Hole; the Tree Hole; Robinson's Bar; the Five Points Hole; and the Black Hole (not a celestial reference, but named for nearby residents). Beyond this twenty-five mile stretch we would have to resort to more descriptive language to designate a specific place. Each of these locations had come to merit a name by yielding a salmon at least once, and most of them from a few fish to many. In addition to this were the places up Yankee Fork, especially the Upper and Lower Falls, as well as the Cliff hole and Third Bridge hole. Sunbeam Dam was the pivot, the gravitational center of action for many summers, even in the years when we camped elsewhere.

At the beginning of our awareness there, salmon were taken exclusively with spears. The commonest method was with a three- or four-pronged, barbed pitchfork mounted on a pole handle about eight feet long. It could be done solo, but usually two or more "fishermen" (hunters) would select a stretch of a small stream in the spawning area perhaps a hundred yards long and, starting at both ends, would converge, wading the stream, poking under cut banks and logs or any other possible cover, and drive the fish out onto a shallow riffle where they could be speared and heaved out onto the bank.

The little store and post office at Sunbeam Dam was run at that time by two brothers, Austin and Dick Lightfoot. They also served, for a modest fee, as fishing guides, and had introduced a salmon spearing method far more sporting and involving much more finesse than the gang-of-pitchforks approach. This made use of a single, bullet-shaped but sharp-pointed harpoon head with a pivoted barb set in a slot in one side. The head was slipped over a metal rod protruding from the thick end of a bamboo pole, and was held in place by a spring or, more commonly, a strip of rubber cut from a tire inner tube. Also attached to the head, and to the pole a foot or so above it, was a piece of clothesline rope about twenty feet long. Once the harpoon head was imbedded in the fish it slipped off the end of the shaft so it wouldn't be torn loose by the leverage of the spear, and the fish was landed by the line. The spear was usually thrust directly into the fish at close quarters, as was the pitchfork; but a rare expert like one of the Lightfoots was known at times to throw the harpoon successfully into a fish passing or lying in shallow water.

About the time we came on the Salmon River scene, another and even more sporting and artistic fishing mode had been developed, I presume by the Lightfoot brothers.

This consisted of snagging the fish, using a treble hook about two inches long and an inch from point to shank, with a three-ounce lead weight soldered to the bottom of it. The hook was tied onto the end of a sixty-pound line on an ocean-type reel and rod. After locating a salmon, one cast the weighted hook beyond and upstream from the fish, worked it into position, and gave a powerful jerk, thereby (hopefully) engaging the hook into the side of the fish at any point along its length. A twenty-pound fish thus hooked and aided by a strong current can go just about anywhere he wants to, despite your persuasion, at least until he tires a bit.

An alternative method, known as blind snagging, required some knowledge of the stream and of the fish's behavior, but less finesse in casting and maneuvering the line. Here one found a place where the fish were known to stop and rest or congregate; cast beyond the spot, let the hook sink, then give a sharp, sweeping motion with the rod. In a large hole you might then let it sink again, reel in a few feet, and repeat the pull once or even twice more; then reel in, cast, and repeat the process; and repeat; and repeat. The fish might or might not be present in their invisible resting place; but the chance of success favored him who, having succeeded once before, believed that they were there and thus was motivated to continue the motions, even hour upon hour.

When Dad first went after salmon he used the harpoon, and Bill and I had our initiation to the hunt with this weapon. I think Dad found the equipment for snagging to be too expensive, or perhaps he felt moved to master one art at a time. Thus the summer we camped at Rough Creek was his season of learning the harpoon and the fish.

He did make one digression, however, an ill-fated departure from standard harpooning. Having read of archery fishing in the tropics, he obtained a simple bow of yew wood, and a half-dozen arrows. He fitted one of our harpoon heads to an arrow, and tried shooting the harpoon-arrow tied to the end of a line wound on a regular casting reel attached to his belt; but there was too much inertia in the reel, and the arrow stopped abruptly on leaving the bow. (The spinning-reel concept hadn't yet reached our part of the world.) After a good deal of experimenting and practice he worked out a method of stripping off several yards of line from the reel, throwing the coils of line on the ground or in the water so they didn't tangle. He practiced on a tree for accuracy. Finally, with the family at a fever pitch of excitement and anticipation, he went one day to the West Fork of Yankee Fork, a small enough stream. As he later told us, he soon saw a salmon moving slowly up a riffle. Making ready his slack loops of line, he took aim and released the arrow. It sailed true on its course, and as it was within a foot of the giant fish there was a searing pain in his left little finger and the arrow dropped dead in the water, stopped by a loop which had whipped up around his hand. The fish moved on upstream, only mildly startled, and Dad gave up forever the hunting of salmon with a bow.

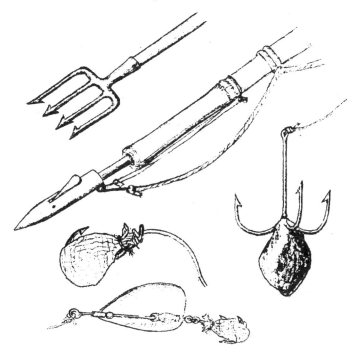

It must have been in about 1932 when someone at Sunbeam Dam was fishing for trout using a large brass spinner with a gob of salmon eggs behind it. To his surprise he caught a chinook salmon. He was surprised because everyone knew that salmon up there don't eat, thus wouldn't strike a bait.

The Lightfoot brothers, being both observant and innovative, promptly fitted a big brass spinner with a cluster of salmon eggs nearly the size of a walnut behind it, on the rig that they usually used for snagging, and discovered that they could catch salmon regularly this way. Thus an entirely new sport was born; the salmon action moved from the shallow spawning areas down into the deeper holes in the main river; and the Lightfoots began selling a new line of gear. Austin seemed to get most of the job of minding the store, while Dick was out on the stream doing research and development.

About two years later it was found that the salmon egg bait worked just as well or with or without the spinner. This was a welcome discovery, as the spinners were expensive and the river was replete with spinner-eating rocks and snags.

After 1934 we retired the harpoons, and the next year the big brass spinners. Thereafter our armamentarium remained constant until about 1942 when snagging became illegal. We would select the method according to location, time, circumstance, and whim: bait fishing with the light to medium outfits in the morning and evening in the main holes along the river and on Yankee Fork; blind snagging with the medium to heavy gear, fifty to ninety pound line with three-ounce weighted hooks at the times when the fish weren't biting; the lighter and medium gear and lighter weights for visual snagging where visibility and accessibility permitted; and the heaviest rods and reels with sixty to ninety pound line for blind snagging in the Upper Canyon on Yankee Fork, where there was no way to follow the fish and the full force of the current in aid of the fish made the terms of the contest non-negotiable.

I have heard it said that in later years salmon have been caught in those waters regularly on artificial lures. On one occasion I tested this out, and in fact caught a salmon on a red and white Andy Reeker wobbler at the foot of the Basin Creek Hole. But this fish was a spawning female, late in the season, in the twilight of her life, and was caught (and released) within a few yards of the spawning bed. Salmon are known to be more touchy and easily aggravated while spawning; I have even seen one seize a naked snag hook as it was retrieved across the gravelly bottom. But whether artificial lures will consistently take fish earlier in their itinerary, I don't know. In any case, we lived in a place and a period which saw an intriguing series of changes in the age-old game of fishing.

BREAKING THE LAW AT THE BIG HOLE

Our parents were good people. My father taught me honor, justice and courage; my mother, kindness, tenderness, compassion. From my father I learned "toughness"; from my mother, "softness". And from each in his or her own way I was taught respect and love for the world, for the out-of-doors, for the way things work. From both I learned honesty, integrity, respect for the law, and patriotism, a love of my country. But my mother also showed me that human dimensions extend across and supersede national and ethnic boundaries. My father gave me Sherlock Holmes, O. Henry, Robert Louis Stevenson, Damon Runyan, and Edgar Allen Poe; my mother, Walt Whitman and Hellen Keller. From my father I was given Scattergood Baines and Tugboat Annie stories in the *Saturday Evening Post*, and my mother led me through a slightly revisionist view of the *New Testament*.

As early as I can remember, it was both explicit when necessary and implicit in all actions of our parents that the law is to be respected and adhered to; that honesty first and respecting the law second are among the cardinal principles of human behavior. (A bad law had to be challenged and corrected – Dad spent his share of time on that – but through legislation, not violation.) A small boy's opportunities for conflict with this code are limited, but among the most common tests we faced in such matters were the fishing regulations. In those days the minimum legal keeping size for trout was six inches, and the daily bag limit was twenty-five fish or fifteen pounds and one fish (this so that if you had fourteen pounds of large fish and caught a two-pounder, you could keep him).

None of us ever knowingly exceeded the limit, though it was permissible as you neared the limit to keep releasing uninjured fish so you could continue fishing. I can remember the shame and anguish of squatting in the sand at dusk, emptying my bag of fish to clean them, and finding that I had miscounted and had twenty-six.

The size was a different matter, a conflict of values which I – and the law – still haven't resolved (in fact only last year I received a warning from a warden for having two under-sized trout in my possession): when an undersized fish is fatally wounded in the process of catching and releasing, it seems morally appropriate to keep the fish and count it against the bag limit. The letter of the law requires that the dismal corpse be returned to the stream; but Dad's teaching on the sin of wanton killing and the waste of game or resources was as strong as that against breaking the law's intent, so the conflict remains. Conflicting values in life abound, fortunately, to keep our moral wits exercised and prevent complacent boredom with our convictions.

The Big Hole (in our Salmon River parlance of 1933), while especially noted for salmon production, also was abundantly supplied with trout. One morning, after the salmon fishing was done for the day, Dad took me to a pair of big partly submerged rocks near the upper end of the hole and introduced me to a new mode of fishing: a fly with a single salmon egg impaled on its hook, dangled into quiet water between the rocks.

Results were rapid; I at once caught a five-inch rainbow. The minimum legal size, as I well knew, was six inches. Dad carefully measured the fish, and then – as a kind of test, of course, since I had caught few fish in my life – asked whether I wanted to keep it or put it back in the water.

I can still feel the struggle of conscience against the desire to show my catch to Mama and to little brother Billy. I finally decided to keep it. I sensed a hidden disappointment in Dad's face as he put the fish in his bag.

A half hour later, when I had caught three more fish, all legal size, the price I had paid was crystal clear. How it would have added to the pride of returning home with the prey if I had released that first one, and shown myself to be maturely law-abiding and above such temptation! But it was too late. As the saying goes, you can only be a virgin once. It was a lesson deeply imprinted in my developing sense of honor and values.

THE MARSH CREEK SUMMER

Our first close acquaintance with The Fish came to pass in the summer of 1934. We camped that summer on Marsh Creek, in the Lolo Creek Campground. It had been carved out of a stand of lodgepole pines, perfect for attaching things: tent guys, clothes lines, orange crate cupboards, a table, a screen cooler, and all the other things one ties, nails, or otherwise affixes to construct a three-month camp. It was our custom in those days to build the car into the camp. using it to support a large shelter tarp. This made it difficult to move, and discouraged us from wearing out the car except on very special occasions.

We had come equipped for the first time to catch salmon, our father having made three of what we called "Indian harpoons." One of these we still have, though the shaft was long ago cut down for more convenient use in lieu of a landing gaff. To our knowledge at that time on the upper Salmon River and its tributaries, there were only two kinds of weapons used against salmon: the "Indian harpoon" and the "pitchfork." Whether the design of the former had actually originated with the Indians I have never known (nor, to my embarrassment, have I made a systematic effort to find out). It had a sharpened tubular steel head with a cleverly slotted and hinged copper barb. The head was held onto a seven-foot bamboo shaft by a light elastic or breakable string, and attached to a line. The head detached from the shaft when the fish was speared, and the fish was played and landed on the line.

For us it was a thrusting weapon. I only knew one man, Austin Lightfoot, expert enough to throw it effectively. His brother, Dick, was undoubtedly of the same class; but we knew him less well.

The "pitchfork" was a standard fish spear with three or four barbed tines, permanently fixed to a shaft like a garden rake handle. Any description of the "pitchfork" must necessarily be sketchy, since none of us would have been caught dead close enough to one to see it in detail. I doubt very much that it mattered to a salmon whether he was speared with a single harpoon and landed on the end of thirty feet of light rope, or was pinioned to the bottom of the stream by a four-tined fork and unceremoniously pitched out on the bank like a shock of hay. Nevertheless, our lips curled in contempt of this crude and cruel barbarism, and we felt ourselves with our harpoons to be, by contrast, veritable benefactors of the fish. This feeling was of a very different order of importance to us from the feelings of superiority that later accompanied growing proficiency with a dry fly. In the latter case, we felt that we were better craftsmen than those around us. In the issue of the harpoon versus the pitchfork, we felt ourselves to be morally superior beings. The pitchfork we came to associate with indiscriminate killing of whatever fish came to hand – spawning females, fish worn past edibility who had earned their historic natural death. We never took such fish, and we used harpoons. The harpoon came to be a symbol of virtue.

When I say "we," I mean our father. I never caught a salmon with a harpoon, though I stalked many, and thrust at a few. Only one of these incidents remains clearly imprinted in my mind – the gravel bar where I stood, the green water over the brown rocks, the partly sub-merged log across an eddy on the far side of the stream, and the wavy yellow-green shadow of a fish fully my own length lying under that log. More than anything in the world at that moment my father wanted me to catch that fish. He was across the stream from me, and had seen it first. He pointed, and I saw it. He motioned me forward, and squatted on the stream bank to watch. I cleared the line, made sure the loop was tight around my wrist – and threw the harpoon. It struck the log, of course. Had it struck the fish, it would hardly have bruised him. The fish circled into the eddy under my father's harpoon, was duly struck and landed. I stood in a miasma of remorse and humiliation that I can feel to this day. I knew when I threw the harpoon that it was the wrong thing to do, that only by a miracle could it work, that I was throwing away a chance in a million, not only to catch the fish but to delight my father. But by then the harpoon, the fish, and the chance were gone.

My brother had a similar but somewhat more satisfactory experience with his first harpooned fish. (I am not certain whether it was his last, but I think that for both of us it would be two more years before we caught our first salmon, after we had graduated to rod and reel.)

It was Ted's day with Dad, mine with Mom. At the time of the great event we were all together, my mother and I watching the fishermen. On the outside of a bend in the stream, the side nearest us, was a large pile of logs that lay against a cut bank in perhaps three or four feet of water. The pile was large enough and solid enough to walk on without disturbing any creature lurking below. It was also an ideal place for a beginner to see fish, since the water between the logs was smooth as glass in places, allowing a clear and undistorted view of the bottom.

Ted, a serious and competent eleven to my uncertain nine, out on the log jam with our father, harpooned a fish right under his feet through the logs. This created a difficulty, since the shaft could not pass through the logs into the open stream, and the opening in the logs was small enough that it was going to be dicey trying to land the fish through it. As it transpired, no solution to the problem was needed; the harpoon head had been fastened to the line with a short length of stovepipe wire, which, after a few fast flexes by the fish, gave way and the fish broke loose.

In the natural course of things, the future of this fish would have been sealed; it had been struck and lost by Ted, his first fish. This made it his. He and Dad, with Mom and me as scouts and assistants, would have hunted it all the rest of the day if need be, and with the other harpoon Ted would eventually have landed it. This implacable pursuit would have been supported also by the fact that the fish had just swum off with one of our three harpoon heads, which were literally irreplaceable.

The natural course of things, however, was not permitted to develop. The fish headed downstream, over a shallow riffle; so shallow, in fact, that his dorsal fin and a bit of his back were out of the water. This made him clearly visible to one Mr. Patterson, a camp neighbor, who was wading up the stream toward us. He promptly impaled the fish with the pitchfork spear he was carrying, and hoisting it aloft, heaved it up on the bank. This scurrilous attack was carried out in the face of our father's furious shouts, "That's the boy's fish!"

We reclaimed the harpoon head and Mr. Patterson kept the fish. After all, no fish marked by four spear tines would ever be permitted to hang from our drying-tree.

In contrast to my first harpoon attempt (a very private experience for my father and myself, its real implications not to be discussed except between ourselves), this experience at the log jam was an encapsulation, a kind of morality play encompassing much that our parents were trying to teach us about living through fishing. On the trail home, over supper that night, and for days to come we discussed, dissected and studied this event for its lessons. Though I have no exact memory of those discussions, they must have included something like the following:

The welded and copper-riveted conviction that pitchfork bearers were immune to the ethics of life in general and of fishing in particular; and that they were no doubt destined to spend eternity in a special hell, impaled on the lances of four-tined swordfish.

The stovepipe wire fastening our harpoon heads to the lines must immediately be replaced with a more suitable material, probably leather thongs.

The catching of fish is only worthwhile if carried out in a manner which takes due regard of all the proper concerns: the fish, the river and countryside, other people, the craftsmanship, the tackle, and the statutes governing fishing; and the relationships among all these: between fisherman and fish, between fisherman and tackle, between fisherman and fisherman, and between fisherman and spectator.

As a consequence of these and similar events over the years our father, in some ways a pure romantic, made of fishing for us a complete ritual, to be observed scrupulously to its finest detail. The objective came to be to fish well in light of the whole ritual, not just in light of the craft; and certainly not just in light of catching fish.

Although the incident of the log jam fish has never been described this way before, I believe it typifies many such events which became display-frames for our parents' values in such a way that they became ours. And so I think of it as one of several Great Events of the Marsh Creek summer.

MOM'S FALL FROM GRACE

It was rare indeed for our gentle little mother to abandon the precepts of the *New Testament* for those of the *Old*. In the camp at Prairie Creek, satisfaction or righteous revenge was what she sought, and what she got.

One end of our camp table was firmly affixed to the trunk of a lodgepole pine. Since the upper branches of this tree touched those of neighboring trees, squirrels could move freely from one tree to another. And one regularly did. He was small, thin, black, and shrill. Every time we sat down to a meal he came from somewhere, ran down the trunk of our tree until he was fifteen feet or so above us; there he would stand on tip-toe, head down, and scream at us as long as we remained at the table. This would elicit various responses from our large black and white dog. Our mother's meals fell short of being the tranquil domestic ceremonies she counted on.

One day Mom detected our noisy little neighbor swiping a dish cloth or some similar bit of kitchen fabric and whisking up the tree with it, presumably for nest material. So she tore a strip of muslin about two feet long and an inch wide from the edge of a dish towel, laid it on the table, and retired to the tent. The squirrel appeared, grabbed this prize, and started up the tree.

The lower trunk of a lodgepole pine has scaly bark, little driddles of pitch in varying stages of dryness, and is studded with dead twig stumps. The cloth strip instantly got caught. The squirrel tugged in vain, then dropped the end of the strip and went down to free the lower end. The upper end caught. He tried the middle. He returned to the upper end. By this time the strip was nearly wrapped around the tree.

I don't know whether that cloth strip ever did reach the nest. I only remember the little squirrel running from one end of it to the other, tugging here and jerking there, chattering in fury around a mouthful of Mother's revenge.

IMPROVISATION

Marsh Creek joins with Bear Valley Creek to form the Middle Fork of the Salmon River. At our Marsh Creek camp in 1934, Bill and I were large enough, at ages nine and eleven, to hold a harpoon, and each of us had a chance or two at a salmon, but neither of us actually landed one. Dad had become quite accomplished with the harpoon (although no match for our constant frame of reference and model of expertise, Dick Lightfoot) and we had salmon to eat. But the thing I remember most vividly about that summer was one of Dad's early ventures in snagging.

He had a fairly light bamboo bait-casting rod and reel with forty-pound-test line, with which he was experimenting with spinner-and-salmon-egg fishing and practicing snagging. John Beckwith, an old schoolmate of Dad's who had never been salmon fishing, came to visit us one day, so Dad fixed the salmon rod for John and improvised another outfit for himself. He tied together two pieces of old trout line, crammed them onto our largest dime-store reel, and mounted the reel on a little telescoping steel rod which was the family's extra (it had been my trout rod until I earned promotion to split bamboo). He attached a small treble hook from a trout lure, and below this on a short piece of wire he suspended some sinkers. Fouling the line on the creek bottom had made inroads recently on our supply of lead, and I clearly recall that the assortment that he had below this hook included two .22 bullets.

As soon as breakfast was over we all set off for the Split Rock Hole, some half-mile down Marsh Creek from camp. Here you could easily wade across a shallow riffle below a deeper area, and come out just below a squarish rock the size of a dining table near the bank. The rock had cracked in two and the pieces separated by about six inches in some prehistoric time; looking down through the crack gave a clear view of the bottom. More than once, down through that crack, Dad had harpooned a salmon that had stopped under the rock to hide and rest.

Today he sent John ahead to check the Split Rock while he searched the riffles above. Nothing was showing in the cleft in the rock, but a hundred yards upstream Dad suddenly saw a fish move up past him and stop in a fast but smooth channel between two rocks that projected just above water. Wading up from below on the far side, he stepped up onto one of the rocks and cast his improvised snag hook upstream. The water was so fast that he couldn't get the hook to sink deep enough before it was swept on past the fish. He must have tried ten or fifteen times – and suddenly he connected.

The fish appeared to take a moment or two to figure out that something was wrong; then it turned and headed lickety-cut down the river, stripping out line of which there was little enough to start with. Dad took off after the fish, jumping off the rock and churning down the middle of the heavy riffle, trying to keep up so as not to come to the end of his line. However, within a few moments it was clear that he was losing the race. As the last turns of line spun off, he reached down and broke the line close to the reel. This maneuver startled and confused me; then I realized that he was hoping to be able to pick up the line again farther downstream.

He staggered out and collapsed on the grass, gasping and almost retching; I had never seen him look so exhausted. The attempt to sprint thirty yards through water up to your hip pockets over slippery rocks that you can't see is no child's play.

After about ten minutes he finally recovered enough to get up, assuring us that he was all right. He moved down below the Split Rock, cautioning us not to make too much commotion. Reasoning that the fish may have gone under the Rock to rest and hide, he waded slowly across the shallow riffle just downstream, dipping in the water ahead of him with the tip of his rod as he went. Sure enough, part way across he brought up the line that had vanished so hastily a few minutes earlier. Carefully pulling it up until he found the free end, he threaded it down through the guides and tied it onto the reel again. He then reeled in until the line drew tight – still unmistakably attached to the fish, and leading under the Rock. Climbing up on the Rock, he looked down through the split and could just see the head of the motionless salmon.

Dad called John over to join him, and after a brief discussion about who should do what, it was agreed that if they were both hooked onto the salmon it would improve the chances of landing it. John anxiously held the rod attached to the fish. Dad took the regular salmon rod in one hand and, lying down on the rock for best vision and control, held the line in the other hand and lowered the hook slowly down beside the fish. Swinging it gently in beside the huge nose, he jerked upward and set the hook just under the edge of the jaw.

The fish surged forward as Dad stood up. Thrashing on the surface a couple of times, it raced upstream, then back down past the fishermen – who by then had noted that John's line hadn't moved. Dad had hooked a different fish! He scrambled down off the rock to follow the new victim, while John held the puny little rod and, dancing up and down, shouted, "Cliff! Cliff! What do I do now? Darn you, Cliff, come back here!"

With the heavier outfit the second fish – a male of about fifteen pounds – was landed after a fight of ten minutes or so. When it was safely out on the bank and subdued, Dad returned to the Rock where John still held the original fish on its leash. With a little coaxing, it now moved rather slowly out from under the rock; having had a light but steady tension against it for a long time now, it was getting tired. This time, with the whole fish in view, Dad snagged it with the heavier outfit (it had become a definite challenge by now to land this one!). It made a last valiant effort, but was soon brought under control and deposited in the huckleberry bushes with the first (or second?) one. Mom, who had happened to look at her watch just as Dad hooked the first fish, announced that the entire capture had taken just an hour and twenty minutes.

The fish was a female weighing twenty-four pounds, and provided exactly a two-quart jar full of eggs – our season's record, and enough to last us for the rest of the summer's fishing. In all of our later exploits, probably no other fish ever equalled this one for a place in legend and memory.

MOM'S FISHING ATTEMPT

During these years of my youth, Dad and Bill and I spent countless hours fishing, during the summer months of camping and on frequent trips of a few hours or a weekend in spring and fall. Our mother never fished. I assumed that she wasn't interested, and can remember only one time when she tried it.

It was on Marsh Creek, where we were camped for the summer. Bill and I persuaded her that she should give it a try, and at a rather likely spot a hundred yards upstream from camp we pressed the rod into her hand, showed her how to hold it and how to operate the reel, and tossed the baited hook out into the riffle. After a few seconds, trying to conceal my impatience with her failure to maneuver the line expertly, I suggested that she lift the bait a bit off the bottom of the stream. The line drew taught, and she put just the right amount of bend in the rod as it met resistance. Her eyes shone with as much excitement as I have ever seen in them as she cried, "I've got one! I've got one!"

It was a stone. As she realized that the hook was snagged on the bottom, her elation faded instantly and was replaced with what I conclude was not so much disappointment as guilt – for doing something wrong, for losing a hook and sinker, perhaps for an untimely display of emotion, or for presuming to step for a moment out of her place into the man's world of fishing. So far as I know, despite our protestations and urgings at the time, she never tried it again.

BULL TROUT LAKE

From Lolo Creek Camp on Marsh Creek, go through the pines past the little stream of drinking water and turn right on the main road, toward Bear Valley and Lowman Pass; but long before you get there turn right at the very unobtrusive sign, BULL TROUT LAKE. A mere mile or less will bring you to a clearing beside the water.

It lay there, dangling its name before us in unspecified promise, conjuring pictures of long, huge-mouthed creatures – mock-trout whose mothers had been scared by a catfish. Our inquiries from natives along the river brought strangely empty answers; we were left, at our first visit there, strictly on our own.

It was our custom that summer, on days not spent at salmon fishing near camp, to take turns and pair up – Dad and Bill, Mom and me, or the other way around – and one pair would decide where we would go today while the other pair planned and packed the lunch. On this day (after long and serious deliberations and conferences) the choices were Bull Trout Lake, and lunch composed of evaporated milk embellished with water, sugar, and vanilla, and topped off with "googumpuckie" sandwiches. There must have been something more, but this all I can attest to with certainty. "Googumpuckie" (Dad's invention, I believe) is cocoa powder, sugar, and milk *quantum sufficit* to make a suitable paste for spreading – a delight for dentists and small boys, and a treat infrequent enough to be memorable in my past.

The lake lay flat and silent under the mid-day sun, and we never saw a fish rise. (Bull trout, or dolly varden, *Salvelinus malma*, are actually a type of charr and tend to be bottom feeders.) There was a nice picnicish spot, of which Mom took charge. A few tentative trials produced no evidence of fish, and after lunch we walked to the head of the lake, to its primary source of nourishment. The little stream tumbled and pranced over some minor rocks and shallows, then slid primly over a light-colored sand bar and into the lake.

Any true mystic must be deeply affected by inlets. Actually, inlets are often good places to fish; and they are invariably good places to fantasize. In the murky residue of my memory this one had it all, the most pure and pregnant of dream-spots. Crystal-clear water, small enough to cross on a half-dozen stepping stones, smoothed out over the pale sand; here and there a half-buried and age-blackened stick provided contrast. The lake bottom, shallow and visible many yards from shore elsewhere, here sloped steeply down into limpid green depths and out of sight. The moving water of the stream was swallowed in motionless darkness, ominous and enticing. Visions of fish – big fish – lurked just beyond that curtain of invisibility, and in retrospect assume a hint of mermaids, or of dragons.

Tense with anticipation, I edged into this obviously superlative fishing spot, while Dad and Bill went on around the lake. My bait vanished into the depths, and languished. Nothing happened. Each cast brought increasing disappointment, even disillusionment. The Underworld had betrayed me, and I finally had to conclude that this was just another part of the lake.

About this time Dad hailed me from a hundred yards or so down the shore, and I joined him and Bill. There was a great tangle of logs, interlaced and crossing one another as if blown down into the lake by some long-forgotten storm. They marked the wide expanse of shallow water into little individual compartments; near the shore some trees hung a few feet above the water, sloping down and outward, but fifty feet out they were all submerged.

Dad had walked out onto one of these logs and had seen, in six or eight feet of water, some fish; when I arrived, he and Bill were already in business. The method was to move very slowly and silently along a log (quietly, so as not to scare

63

the fish, but sitting down, so as not to scare Dad) and drop a single salmon egg on a #16 hook with a fine leader on the other side of a submerged log where the fish were hidden from our view and vice versa.

The fish were not large, but were numerous – all bull trout, about seven to ten inches. I suppose we caught twenty among us before they became reluctant, we had plenty for the frying pan, and the lengthening shadows beckoned us to the car.

I'm still sure, however, that the lake's true secrets lie at the inlet in that deep, mysterious green water.

MORE ON THE MARSH CREEK SUMMER

The Marsh Creek summer of 1934 was, for our mother, the best of them all. I didn't know this until years later, when she told me. I knew at the time that she was happy, though; it was later that all three of her men sort of lost track of her. Mom loved to hike. She wore jodhpurs and high-laced boots and carried a small back pack. She was a miniature; her hundred pounds was fit into four feet eleven, and she held the trail down with size four-and-a-half boots. A lovely lady, our mother. But she loved to hike, and to climb mountains. This Dad failed completely to understand. Why work like the devil to get somewhere you don't have any good reason to be? In this, of course, he was wrong-headed to the point of bigotry. And to this day I share his view.

But during the Marsh Creek summer Mom got away with it. Nearly every day, Ted and I took turns. One went fishing with Dad; and one went hiking, berry picking, picnicing, animal watching, or mountain climbing with Mom. My clearest memory of these ventures is my mother sitting on a hillside in the shade of a big pine tree, doing cut-work embroidery on a linen tablecloth. That is what she carried in her little backpack all that summer – her embroidery and our lunch. I still have that tablecloth and napkin set, with its thousands upon thousands of sunlit stitches. It is my one tangible object from that summer.

Often we would agree on some spot along the river where we would all meet in the afternoon and walk back to camp together. It was always exciting to see what the fishermen had been up to. (I'm afraid it was not as exciting to see the huckleberries or other fruits of the hikers' day. Mom's was a losing battle. When it comes to romance, roots and berries just don't make it.) Meeting places were always fishing holes with their special names. I don't remember many of these from Marsh Creek. Only two, the Split Rock Hole and the Log Jam, remain clear in my mind. The name, though not the look, of a third, where I missed my first salmon, is gone. But in all the later years, wherever we camped, landmarks were always fishing holes given proper names.

As it dominated our geography, fishing gradually dominated our summer lives. The Marsh Creek summer started the salmon fishing, and the salmon gradually narrowed our mother's days. More and more often, Ted and I both went fishing with Dad; and more and more Mom became a spectator, going along to be a gracious audience, or staying to be a gracious camp keeper. By 1938 her three males were working as commercial fishing guides, and most days she was alone. Writing, I found out years later: poetry, plays, stories. She would put away her notebook and praise our catch and serve supper.

SECTION THREE

Back to Bigger Water
and
Bigger Deeds
On Salmon River

MY FIRST SALMON

In 1935, when I was twelve, Dad's success at salmon fishing had become well established, and he began to devote a considerable amount of time and effort to see that Bill and I got into the act as well. I had learned to handle a casting outfit pretty well, and helped with landing Dad's fish several times, but it was well into the season before I connected with a salmon myself. At a small but previously productive hole on a bend three or four miles up Yankee Fork, I finally drifted the bait through the deep place to the satisfaction of the salmon, who took it in the typical rather casual fashion of a chinook seizing a gob of salmon eggs for some as yet mysterious reason. I set the hook properly, and it was at once apparent that it was a fish of decent size for eating but of very modest proportions as salmon go, a "jack" (the small males who have gotten their calendars or their glands mixed up, or just got tired of waiting for adult-hood, and have come up from the sea to spawn in two or three years instead of the standard four). It weighed probably six or seven pounds, and fought valiantly enough for its size but was not hard even for me to subdue. Dad offered to help land it, but since it was my first, I suddenly felt very possessive and declined the offer. (I sensed that Dad was a bit hurt, but in the flurry of the moment I may well have misread his expression.) After a few minutes of following the fish down into the next riffle and leading it across to my side, I landed it by hand and waded back up with it to the admiring audience of father and brother.

It was fun, and I tried to find the appropriate balance between pride and modesty. Secretly I was a little disappointed that my first one was not a big, feisty fish that would have made for a more heroic tale in the telling later.

We had some salmon on hand for food already, and Mom, after suitable exclamations, suggested that maybe I would like to give the fish to Cap Sebree, the miner, prospector, and legendary old-timer who lived in a little cabin not far from ours. With a twinge of selfish regret (not even to taste my first salmon?) I cheerfully agreed, and carried the fish through the cool pines to where Cap's place backed up against the hill. He was sitting motionless in front of his house in an old chair made of pine branches, so that he and the chair and the cabin and the spots of sun splashing through the lodgepoles onto the needle-padded ground all seemed to be integral parts of a single pattern.

I paused shyly until he turned his head, and made my presentation. It was the first time I had ever spoken personally to Cap, and I waited, awed by his venerable presence. Visions swam in my head of the gourmet delights that he would create with this wondrous fish. Mom always fried or baked the salmon, and it was fine eating; but after all, some said Cap was French, and don't the French do magic in the kitchen?

Cap peered at the fish in silence for a full minute, it seemed; then he said tersely, "Good! I'll boil the bugger."

I handed him the fish and walked slowly home, reflecting on this ignominious end for my first salmon.

OF VISUAL SNAGGING AND
ONCOHRYNCHUS NERKA

Of all the fishing we did, visual snagging was to me the highest art. It combined more sophisticated aspects of the craft than any other form. With great regret we gave it up in the early 1940s, because it became illegal in the State of Idaho, caught in a blanket prohibition on taking salmon on unbaited hooks without lures. Forgive the legislators, for they knew not what they did. By 1941 the number of people skilled enough to take salmon this way were a small group all of whom we knew well. Dick Lightfoot was the acknowledged master, and when he made one of his rare visits to the river we would make every effort to watch him fish. (He was unique in this; no one else could thus lure us from our own fishing.) His brother, Austin; the three of us; our uncle, Howell Leyson; Howard Davis and his son Dodger, who ran the store at Sunbeam; Fred, a free-lance guide whose last name escapes me; Max Yost, our closest fishing buddy; these and not more than two others might have been expected to succeed in snagging a sockeye, or a chinook in deep water, except by chance.

Perceiving more to salmon fishing than harpooning, our father began visual snagging on Marsh Creek in 1934. He robbed spinners of their three-pronged hooks, hung weights close below them, and set out to find ways to catch fish. For these earliest attempt he spliced together a couple of worn fly lines, and with them armed an old telescoping steel rod. (As a consequence of this eccentricity, it was at one time being rumored in the nearby settlement of Stanley that some nut on Marsh Creek was fishing for salmon with flies.) With this equipment, only the most rudimentary casting was possible. Dad's success almost always depended on finding a fish with some bit exposed into which he could sink the hook, holding the line in his hand. The Split Rock and several other spots were well suited to this strategy, since they permitted the fisherman to stand directly above the intended victim.

This primitive tackle yielded some splendid results. One Split Rock fish, a huge male chinook, took two hours to land. In all the following years none of us ever caught one as large. After being cleaned and hung overnight, wrapped in a bedroll and taken one hundred miles to Mountain Home, it was weighed into John Beckwith's frozen food locker at twenty-nine pounds. In the water it must have exceeded forty.

Another time Dad snagged the same fish three times. His determination was in part a matter of economics. The fish was not large, but extraordinarily red in color for a chinook. Dad hooked it, and it promptly broke his line. He put on another hook, found the fish, and hooked it again. Again it broke his line. By this time it was carrying around two-thirds of his tackle, making it absolutely imperative that the third and last attack succeed. After a lengthy search the fish was again located, this time succumbing to its fate and yielding back to Dad the treasure it bore in its hide.

By 1937 we had good Calcutta rods, casting reels, and good lines, and visual snagging had taken on new dimensions. We continued assaulting chinook in this fashion when the occasion arose, but practiced it most seriously against sockeyes. These we considered to be the prince of fish, *Oncorhynchus nerka* to the chinook's *Oncorhynchus tshawytscha..* Where we met them in the river they were more than a thousand miles from their last meal, but still a long way from their terminal rites of spawning. They were sleek and fast, and furious surface fighters. Their coloring, like that of other anadromous fish, varied considerably, depending on their physiological proximity to spawning. With the sockeye, a red stripe along the midline of each side from gills to tail increased in width and intensity with advancing maturity. Thus on the first fish of the season the red marking was barely visible, while on later ones it was dominant.

A typical sockeye would be perhaps twenty-two inches long and weigh four or five pounds. Its back would be a dark blue-green, devoid of spots. The head would be a sharply contrasting brighter and purer green. The dark color of the back blended into the red center stripe, which in turn blended into the silvery white belly.

Illustrations in the books show the sockeye with a pronounced hump behind the head and a hooked nose. I never observed these features. Late in the season a large male might exhibit a trace of each, but nothing like the pictures. Perhaps the pictures are confined to specimens which are very near spawning; or perhaps the race of *O. nerka* that comes to the upper Salmon River differs somewhat from others, for example those that spawn in the Fraser River watershed in British Columbia. I don't know. In any case, they were glorious fish, and their first appearance in the big hole at Sunbeam Dam in late July or early August was one of the most exciting events of the summer.

The tackle we used for sockeyes was derived from that which we saw Dick Lightfoot using, with some refinements of our own. We used the rods, reels, and lines that served in bait casting for chinook, but the end tackle was unique. It consisted of about six feet of 25-pound test leader, and a number one or two treble hook. Six to ten inches below the hook was a long thin two-ounce weight. Where the leader tied to the line, we would attach a bit of white rag for visibility. To our mother's sorrow, these little flags commonly were hems torn from our handkerchiefs. She never could understand why we couldn't sentence one whole handkerchief to this fate, instead of tearing a corner or two from every one we owned.

By the time I was twelve I knew all the knots in the Boy Scout Handbook except the long splice (which I still don't know), so assembling this tackle was no problem. Catching a fish with it was something else. Sockeyes were remarkably uncooperative in this. They were spooky and quick, in this respect resembling trout more than salmon. Moderately gregarious, they seemed to stay in groups of from three to five, and were more or less constantly on the move. They rode well up off the bottom and would drift from place to place, disappearing for a time in the deep fast water, then playing tag in a big circle through the shallows.

Though sockeyes were occasionally caught elsewhere, the big hole at Sunbeam Dam best met the requirements of this highly specialized fishing. It was large, with water deep and shallow, fast and still. The river entered it through a deep chute, difficult enough for the fish that they were tempted to rest for a day before moving on. Above it was a cliff, adorned by a fragment of the old concrete fish ladder, on which we could stand and look down some fifteen feet at a good angle for seeing the fish. From this small platform a somewhat precarious trail led around a shoulder of the cliff and down to the gravel beach below, where fish could be landed. The twenty-some square feet of this concrete-and-rock fragment was famous along the river as The Ledge, and was the fishing spot by far the most in demand for forty miles in either direction.

To describe this hole it is necessary to convey some idea of the size and volume of the river, and how does one do that? It was large enough that its riffles were justly called rapids. One had to go twelve miles above Sunbeam Dam to find a place where the river could be waded at low water. A heavy rapids might average six feet deep and be forty yards wide. The river was rough enough and crooked enough that if a hooked fish was fifty yards from the fisherman, the odds were good that it was out of sight around a corner or rock outcrop. It was necessary in some places to cast fifty yards to reach a good spot. It was totally devoid of boats. Depths in excess of fifteen feet were common. What more can I say? It was a big, rough, rowdy river. Standing on The Ledge, one faced directly across the river perhaps fifty yards toward a huge, steep gravel bank. Forty yards to the right the green water squeezed into a twenty-foot cut in the solid rock, tilted down a fifteen-foot drop in the river bed. Near the bottom the smooth surface of the fall was churned to white froth as the current turned a bit against jagged rocks and roared straight through the pool below. A narrow eddy lay on the near side against the cliff face. On the far side the circling current had washed out the gravel bank in a great curve, scooping room for a deep and wide eddy in which at certain stages of water one could keep a bait circling indefinitely. At the lower end of the hole the river split against a low, rocky island into two heavy channels, about one third of the volume of the river rushing down the near side and two thirds on the far side.

During the sockeye season we could commonly be found standing on The Ledge at first light, gazing fixedly into the black water, hoping for that glimpse of wavy shadows that would announce the presence that morning of The Fish. If they were not there, we would go to casting for chinook. If they were there, we were faced with a difficult decision: should we try for them at once, and risk scaring them into deep water before it got light enough for a clear view; or should we wait for brighter daylight, and risk the chance that some other fisherman might horn in on our act? The three of us would draw straws, long straw making the first try.

The problem was one of drifting the weighted hook to an exact spot some four feet below the surface of fast-moving water, and knowing when it got there without being able to see it; all this while the spot to be reached was swimming (with luck, slowly) somewhere else. One had first to cast to a point upstream and beyond the fish, such that a) the fish would not be scared off by the splash; and b) the angle of line and current would permit maneuvering the hook to the fish. I suppose that I made fifty such casts over two seasons before approaching the kind of automatic and instant judgement of current, depth, angle, refraction (a fish seen under four feet of water is in fact a considerable distance from where it appears to be) and hook weight, necessary to success.

If the cast was off, the trick was to detect this soon enough to get out of the way without scaring the fish. Then middle straw would try. (Let us say that Dad, an incurable romantic, had rigged the draw to give me, the youngest, the first shot, Ted the second, and himself the third.) Ted would then have a go. The cast; the careful maneuvering of the hook toward the fish, seeing only the white rag on the black line; the cast good, the line of approach true; a quick jerk – just too soon. One fish darts up and out into white water, the rest follow, and the first round of the day is over. (Had Dad drawn the long straw, he would not have fully enjoyed the silver and red-blue prize that would have been stashed in the cold shade of a rock below. By the end of the second season he had stopped rigging the draws.)

Sometimes we kept watch all day for reappearances of the sockeyes, eating in shifts, knowing that two hours of careful watching might produce one fleeting chance. If other fishermen showed up, we would turn to bait casting for chinook. People rarely learned of the presence of the sockeyes without being shown, and that kind of fishing we didn't care to advertise. We never included it in our guiding, and to the day it became illegal, tried to keep it in a small circle of family and close friends. It was a craft too difficult and too valuable to be casually shared.

By 1937 the salmon fishing had become the center of our summer busyness, and the object of some of our most serious spring preparations. These included a trip to Twin Falls as soon as we heard that Gerrish Hardware had received their annual shipment of rod material. This consisted of a hundred or so sticks of what was referred to as "Tonkin cane" or "Calcutta bamboo." It was a reddish, thick-walled bamboo with closely spaced joints and came, we were told, from the Tonkin district of Indochina, later part of North Vietnam. It was wonderfully strong and made superb salmon rods. These often broke sometime during the second year of use, so new ones were required every summer. These rods even collapsed with panache; one day a rod would survive a thirty-minute tussle with a large and stubborn fish. The next, the rod's owner would set the hook in response to a strike and find himself holding two feet of butt, the rod having broken at virtually every other section. This would allow those sections which carried guides to slide down the line to the hook – or perhaps to a ten-inch trout which had been responsible for the strike.

We hoped each year to have first pick from Gerrish's new supply. We would carry the bundle of bamboo into the alley behind the store and go through the entire lot. We would eliminate them down to a dozen or so, choosing for straightness, and appropriate weight. Then each of us would painstakingly pick one. This choice was supremely important. Each would have to live with his choice of rod as long as it survived, not only using it but fiercely defending its virtues as superior to any other rod in history. It would be named, and distinctively decorated. Its first and its largest fish would be duly noted. Its sensitivity; its casting capabilities, including the amount of lead needed to achieve maximum distance; its success in meeting the extra demands in snagging sockeyes; its records of missed strikes; in all these ways and others, each rod would be pitted against its mates until it too slid in pieces down the line. So the ceremony behind Gerrish's Hardware was a solemn affair, partaking somewhat of the air of a wedding.

When each had chosen for better or for worse, Dad would pick out a couple more for utility, loan, and emergency; we would pay a dollar each for the lot, select the necessary hardware, and depart for home.

The next stage was the decision of each as to where to cut our rods – how much to take off of butt and tip. The goal was to end up with the lightest, softest rod commensurate with its challenges. Each was eager to conclude that he should leave the thinnest tip, for after all, had he not chosen the strongest and best stick?

When finished, the rods were identical from the black crutch tip on the butt to about six inches above the reel seat. Beyond that point they tended to differ only in appearance, not in cosmic principle. If one decided to whip his rod with colorful fly-rod silk thread, decorating the spaces between the guides and marking off a rule above the reel; then the next, with contemptuous sneer, would decide on basic black for whipping, with not one turn of thread more than necessary to secure the guides. One was, after all, constructing a weapon, not a showy toy. (This was my favorite ploy, since it allowed me to finish my rod long before Ted, a patient and meticulous workman, could finish his.)

These rods were six and a half to eight feet long, in one piece, and carried six or seven bell guides (the cheapest good ones) and a hardened tungsten tippet. The butts were whipped with carpenter's yellow chalk line for something over two feet, with the reel seat inserted about eighteen inches from the butt. They were equipped with medium grade but small level-wind casting reels and fifty yards of thirty-pound-test Black Ghost braided silk line. With them you could cast an ounce and a half of weight and bait fifty yards with luck – and delicacy of touch with thumb on spool – and they would easily stand the strain of breaking that line against the spring of the rod. With use and age they tended to accumulate a substantial bend, which we never tried to straighten, considering it a sign of prowess.

To my knowledge only one of these rods has survived. An indomitable piece of wood, it joined the arsenal in 1941. It was used continuously for two seasons by me, four more by our father, then in various other waters for twenty more. For its last catch it was in the hands of my son's wife, Barbie. She and my venerable rod took a twelve-pound ling cod in Stuart Channel off Vancouver Island. It (the rod, not the cod) is now in honorable retirement on my ceiling.

THE OLD ROAD

My first memories of Salmon River are largely those of the road and the strip of world that lay beside it. From Ketchum up along Wood River was a good gravelled road, dusty and with "washboard" surface in places but easily wide enough to meet and pass a car anywhere. Leaving the valley and climbing toward Galena Summit it made a series of switch-backs or "hairpin turns", sharp and steep. In most places you could pass a car except on the turns, where one car might have to back a few yards and wait at a turnout while the other went by.

Dad told of driving a sheep truck over Galena a few times and finding one or two of the curves too sharp for the truck to crank around in one movement; he had rather to enter the curve, back sharply toward the steep outside edge, then forward, then back around again before the body of the truck could clear the bank on the inside of the curve. Once during this maneuver he got a rear wheel over the edge. Afraid of rolling the truck down the mountain and injuring a lot of sheep, he ended up building a corral on the mountainside out of downed lodgepoles and branches, and unloading all of the sheep (carrying each one in his arms to the pen) before jacking and blocking up the wheel to get it back on the road. Though traffic was very light in those days, I can nevertheless picture quite a few helpers or watchers gathered on either side of him by the time he was loaded up and on his way again.

Over the summit and through the woods and down the other side the road was the same, a good wide one-lane road where, by slowing down and using some care, two cars could pass in most places. Twenty miles farther on, however, following the Salmon River as the valley narrowed toward Stanley, the road was a bit more economical, a one-lane track with frequent turnouts, and the next sixty miles or so, all the way to Challis, was like this. The road surfaces – dirt, lightly gravelled – were quite well maintained, by standards of that day, and the edges overhanging the river were well rocked up and pretty secure except after especially heavy weather; still, it was none too wide for comfort. I remember Nanan, our paternal grandmother, riding with Papa in their old Model A Ford, her face and her knuckles white as she clutched the edge of the window while he negotiated those switchbacks over Galena and the places where the thread of a road was cut into the mountain far above the river.

We camped one summer just beside the road at Rough Creek, about four miles up river from Sunbeam Dam. Half a day might pass sometimes without a car passing, and more than once an urban traveller stopped at our camp to inquire nervously how much farther the road was like this. We always felt a certain snobbish amusement at this, for to us it was just an ordinary road.

One morning Dad and Bill and I had been fishing below Sunbeam and were headed back up-river toward breakfast. Along this stretch the road hugged the river almost every foot of the way, with a steep hill above the road, and there was no possibility of passing except at the turnouts provided. In most cases these were spaced closely, every couple of hundred yards or so. Some of them, though, were farther apart, and in one place it was exactly a mile between turnouts. As we entered this mile we met a car; Dad backed to the turnout we had just passed, exchanged waves as the other car went by, and proceeded. At about the halfway point we met another car; heaving a sigh, and muttering something about the buckwheat cakes and coffee waiting for us, Dad waved at the other driver and backed the half mile to the turnout.

Starting out the third time we eagerly scanned each turn of the road, sure that there couldn't be such a traffic jam as to bring us yet another encounter. We relaxed as we passed the half-mile point, for now it would be up to the other driver to do the backing.

Just as we came within sight of the next turnout we saw another car coming. It pulled in toward its left, nestling as tightly to the vertical rocky bank as possible, and stopped. Six feet to its right was the edge of the road, and ten feet below that was murmuring water. We saw that there were two ladies in the car, and they didn't look happy.

Pulling up facing them, Dad stopped and waited. Nothing happened. He got out and went over and greeted them pleasantly; it turned out that they were school teachers from New Jersey, on their first trip out West and terrified of this road. Dad explained that there was a place a mere fifty yards behind them where we could pass, whereas it would be a mile in the other direction to a passing spot; he politely asked the lady if she would mind backing up that short way.

She would mind very much.

In that case, Dad would be glad to back her car to the turnout for her. But no thank you, she was not at all interested in this offer; she sat clutching the wheel and seemed prepared to wait there all day, if need be, for this obstacle to disappear.

After another gentle and fruitless appeal, Dad got into the car, backed up one mile to the wide place, and waited. It seemed like a quarter of an hour before the ladies drove by; the driver gave a wan smile and nod, but couldn't afford to take a hand off the wheel to return our waves.

As we finally made our uninterrupted way home we discussed the pity of such under-privileged people, so habituated to wide flat roads as to lose, in a flood of fear, all the joy of a beautiful drive down the Salmon River.

LLEW CLAWSON

Standing on The Ledge at Sunbeam Dam you could see, all but hidden behind the hill, the chimney and the corner of the rusty iron roof of Llew Clawson's house. After fishing since first light, we would stand cold and shivering and watch that chimney. At about the time the sun touched the treetops beyond the mouth of Yankee Fork, the first wisps of smoke would rise. We would wait another twenty minutes and then go down to join Llew for a cup of the most incredibly thick, muddy, delicious coffee and the cozy warmth of his kitchen.

Llew (Llewellyn) was born, I think, in Nebraska, when his parents, Calvin and Czarina Clawson, were publishers of the *Omaha Bee*. He came in his youth with his parents and spent most of his life in Bonanza, Idaho. In the heyday of the gold mining era in the late 1800s he was prospector, merchant, Justice of the Peace, and assayer of gold ore, among other things. Later he was watchman at the power plant of the Golden Sunbeam Mining Company. Early in the twentieth century, when the price of gold had fallen and the pursuit of gold had lost some of its profit and glamor, the Sunbeam, Lucky Boy, General Custer, and other mines up Yankee Fork had closed down and the ore-processing mill at Custer no longer had any business. The power plant at Sunbeam Dam fell idle, but for several years the company continued to pay Llew to watch over its rusting remains. Finally it was dismantled and taken away for salvage, and the Golden Sunbeam Mining Company went out of existence, leaving Llew in possession of the little three-room watchman's house that had been his home for many years.

He was a quiet, gentle, spinstery sort of gentleman. His Smokey Bear hat, his sparse hair, and his freckles seemed all the same color, a brownish gray with a hint of bygone reddish days. Given sufficient time and priming he could

produce a wealth of stories about the past, and our mother –
who never fished – spent many a summer afternoon amid the
drone of the flies, the breeze in the pines outside, and Lew's
soft and hesitant voice recalling the early days of Custer and
Bonanza.

The summers of our acquaintance with Llew moved by
like the pendulum of a grand-father clock. One mid-winter our
mother awoke, she told us, at three in the morning, for no
apparent reason. She went to the window, and as she looked
out she saw a sleigh move silently across the moonlit field of
snow in front of our house. She was almost sure it was Llew
riding in the sleigh.

After sunup she made a couple of phone calls, and
learned that Llew had been sick and in the hospital down-river
in Challis for three days, and had died early that morning.

She also found that, having no remaining relatives or
close friends, Llew had written a will leaving all his
possessions to our parents. His "estate" consisted of the house,
an old Model A Ford, three mining claims, some gold scales
and other assayer's equipment, and an unquantifiable amount
of old records, letters, photographs, books, diaries, journals,
and family keepsakes.

Some of this material has been placed in the historical
archives of the State of Idaho; some lost or discarded; and
some integrated into our own family accretion of lore and
artifacts. The old house, which we used in the summers for the
next eight years, has been torn down. But in many ways Llew
lives on, and remains most sharply in my memory as the gentle
elf, fussing so graciously over his steaming and viscous coffee
in his little island of warmth at dawn.

SALMON EGGS, ECONOMICS, POLITICS

Obviously the primary purpose in the life of a female salmon (if you embrace the idea of "purpose" in this way) is to carry a quart and a half of eggs a thousand miles into fresh water and cover them with a thin layer of gravel.

Our purpose, on the other hand, in pursuing salmon eggs was to use them to catch other salmon. There's a cosmic paradox here which I'll not pursue further, preferring instead the other cosmic question seldom voiced but often pondered: why would a salmon, male or female, near the end of its journey and with a totally inert digestive tract, strike a gob of salmon eggs? Certainly not for food. No other bait or lure worked. The eggs worked, whether or not attached to a spinner; the spinner alone was useless. Is it anger? Envy? Some subtle hormonal magnetism? A deeply subconscious response to the scent? The question hits the wall in my mind.

Whatever the reason, in a day of avid fishing we might use a few ounces of eggs, so the capture of a twenty-pound female in her full ovulatory glory was an occasion for rejoicing. The problem was that we had no refrigeration, and the eggs would spoil before we could use them up; not to mention the matter of catching that first female.

In those years the Sunbeam Store and Post Office was run by Howard Davis and his son Dodger. It was a marginal operation, and Howard supplemented his income any way he could. During the months of winter when there was almost no business, Howard made little boxes and chests and chess boards finely inlaid with exotic woods.

In spring, at high water, whitefish came to the river in abundance, and Dodger harvested an ample supply. Howard smoked them, and through the summer these salty little snacks were laid out on a tray near the store entrance, free for the taking; he had found that this significantly enhanced his sale of bottled soda pop which lay in a crate of ice nearby.

85

Another bit of extra revenue was in the preservation and sale of salmon eggs. If a fisherman brought him the eggs from a salmon, he would preserve them with his secret formula, so they would keep and retain much of their fresh character for weeks. In exchange for this service he would keep half the eggs to sell to someone else. The arrangement was fair enough, but sometimes we had to buy back some of the eggs that we had caught, and especially when fishing was not being very productive, we thought covetously of that other half of the eggs.

One day Dad had caught a good fish, and Bill and I took the eggs in for treatment. We watched Howard use a jar with holes in the lid to sprinkle the contents – which looked like table sugar – onto the eggs, carefully separating each of the crosswise layers of membrane so the chemical reached all the eggs.

Bill noticed, in the wastebasket under the meat cutting block, a tin can. It was smaller than a two-pound coffee can; it had some printing on it but the main part of the label wasn't visible. As we left with our share of the eggs, Bill was smiling, and when we got outside he chuckled.

"I know the secret recipe!" he said.

Our grandfather and uncle were professional photographers, and Dad had learned enough of the skills to do the photography for the school yearbooks. At that time a photographer was also an alchemist, weighing out and mixing the ingredients for his developing solutions for the darkroom, and Bill and I had plenty of experience in this.

"I'll bet there's only one chemical that comes in a can that size and shape." he said. "That's sodium sulfite."

From then on we preserved our own eggs. We eventually explained to Howard how we discovered his secret, and promised not to tell anybody else; but thereafter we enjoyed the full measure of the gift from the lady fish.

AUTUMN COMES

I had fished up Yankee Fork all the way to Eight Mile Creek. Glints of golden light danced on the broken surfaces of the water that splashed, gurgled, and gushed toward me. I could feel my pant legs gently flapping to the pull of the current, and the sugar sack of fish, hung precariously by two large safety pins, dragged heavily at my belt.

A rumble, felt more than heard, came from deep in the channel where the main thrust of the river met two giant boulders and was forced aside. This bass line was overlaid by tenors and altos from the riffle above, and high-pitched grace notes of a spring trickling in from the left bank filled out the orchestration in a mystical minor key. Pine scent was in the breeze, but had to compete with the fragrance of fish that clung to my sticky fingers despite repeated rinsings.

Carefully shifting my balance, I edged up to the tail of the riffle, ragged tennis shoes feeling for footing among the slippery green and brown rocks. My feet, numb from the cold water and the scouring of sand in my socks, were sluggish in obeying commands.

Twice I had stopped on the bank to count my fish, and knew I was just one short of the limit. In no hurry to finish, I cast the fly to promising spots, squinting to follow its progress among bubbles and swirls and the blinding little flashes of reflected sun. A delicious fatigue in my shoulder attested to endless cast-and-retrieve, cast-and-retrieve to make the lure follow the flow convincingly. Almost too soon a white belly flashed, the fly swirled from view, and soon a nine-inch cutthroat had joined its kin in my sugar sack.

I stood for a few moments, savoring the feel of the place, then reluctantly turned away. Carefully threading my rod ahead of me, I crawled through the salmon berries and wild roses that separated the stream from the steep hillside, and engaged in brief combat with tangled branches and miniature thorns; then, using hands and feet, I scrambled up the shale slope.

Standing at last on the flat, I was aware of stillness. My ears, tuned earlier to the noise of the river and then to the hillside clatter of rocks, heard quiet.

I started slogging down the road to where the car would be waiting. Then I stopped again.

I've never been able to define it. I try to think like a scientist, but it doesn't help. Never mind astronomers and almanacs. Autumn comes of its own bidding, when it's ready, and when it comes I know it.

It's probably something in the air, but I don't know which of my senses tells me. I've thought it was the temperature, or the light, or the sounds and the way the wind brushes my face; but on careful study, none of these checks out.

The sunlight flowing now from near the west rim of the canyon seemed thin and delicate, a tracery of gold on the treetops around me. As I listened, the silence peeled away in layers. I heard again the rush of the river, now faint in the bottom of the canyon. Then that tissue-paper sound that a breeze makes in moving through lodgepoles. Another layer stripped away, and a pine squirrel chattered at great distance. Finally I was aware of my own breathing.

And that feeling. I didn't understand it, but I knew with certainty that in that moment the world had changed.

Back at the car, I asked my mother whether she had noticed it. She said yes, it was a beautiful afternoon, in a lovely place; and yes, autumn was coming on. She meant it, and was enjoying it, all right; but I knew from the way she answered that she had missed it, that she hadn't experienced what I had. It was a different thing altogether, and something I couldn't share.

It happens, of course, wherever I happen to be, and I've been a lot of places at ends of summers. Some years I miss it entirely. Sure, the daytime shadows are getting longer and nights may be getting cooler, but I can't actually feel the earth tilt. I just eventually look around me and see, from frost and fallen leaves and pumpkins, that fall has been here for a while.

The other day I came outside thinking of something important and before I got to the parking lot it hit me, stopped me dead in my tracks – that same old startling event, an atmospheric condition or something inside my chest, or the Spirit of such things laying a hand on my shoulder.

Even now, in my waning years, I can't explain it and don't know what to name it. But I can tell you this: autumn came this year on September eighth at eleven o'clock in the morning under cloudless skies.

CAP SEBREE AND A SUNRISE BREAKFAST

In a one-room cabin on the flat behind the Sunbeam Store lived an old gentleman known to us as Cap. I consider it an extraordinary privilege that Cap's generation and mine overlapped, however meagerly, for Cap was truly a man of the romantic frontier. Our grandfathers were too, of course; but they were farmer-photographer and farmer-minister, and we knew them in houses and towns, pursuing their modern ways. Not so Cap. He lived in a grey-weathered log cabin, just like the abandoned trappers' cabins we could see along the old trails-turned-mountain roads. He had drunk in the saloons of the ghost towns we knew. He had been a miner in Custer, five miles up Yankee Fork, back when it was still an actual living town. He had driven freight wagons, hauling ore to the railroad in Ketchum, sixty-five miles away over a mountain pass. He had been in the Klondike; rumor had it that he got the name "Cap" from running a freight boat on the Yukon.

He taught Ted and me to use a gold pan, to build a sluice box, and how to get the clean gold out of the final concentrate in the bottom of the pan. He showed us how mercury would collect all the tiny bits of gold out of a cup of black sand, and then could be safely vaporized off and recaptured under a hollowed-out half of a potato, leaving a lump of gold-and-mercury amalgam on the stove top.

"Never do it that way myself," he said. "I've got all winter, so I dry the black sand and gold in the oven, dump it in the pan, and blow the sand off. Like to see the gold in a poke. You boys probably don't have patience enough to do that." He was right; but he taught us respect for his craft: if you don't take the time to do it right, the gold goes out with the gravel.

He didn't tell stories. He just hinted at them, and let us fill in details with our wide-eyed imaginings. He left the impression that his life had been far too rough to share with innocent children.

"Leave the whiskey alone, boys," he would say. "Seen it ruin too many men right here in Custer." And I would see Cap, old as I knew him, standing sadly in a Custer saloon, head and shoulders above the drink-crazed miners ruining themselves around him.

"Teach us to play poker, Cap."

"Oh, no, boys. You don't want to learn that game. It can take everything you've got." And I would see Cap in that same saloon, shaking his head at the folly of those whose gold he was winning.

As with other parts of these reminiscences, it is impossible to know what is memory and what are the embellishments of time and telling. But with Cap, I know memory has built legend; I just don't know exactly where the boundaries are. Sometimes I wish I could be sure. I would really like to know who and how many sat down to breakfast with Cap one morning at sun-up. I'll tell it as I remember it, which, after all, is Cap's gift to me.

He invited Ted and me to breakfast with him, instructing us to come early – after day-light, but before the sun hit the mountain across the canyon. When we arrived, he opened the cabin door flat against the wall, and pushed a table against the opening. He set places for Ted and me in the shadows at the ends of the table, and for himself opposite the door.

"Sit down there and be quiet," he told us. We did, moving only our eyeballs as we watched him set the table and serve the pancakes. As breakfast proceeded, other guests began to arrive. A camp robber (known elsewhere as a grey or Canada jay), a golden-mantled ground squirrel, a golden chipmunk or two, a junco, all joined in the pancake feast. The bolder ones, like the camp robber, ate off of Cap's plate. The more timid were served at the open door. Us, they ignored.

The repast finished and the table cleared, we walked home, chastened. Yes, Cap took the time to do things right.

91

HUNTING SALMON IN THE CANYON

The Upper Falls on Yankee Fork, just above Five Mile Creek, is a spectacular and exciting place to be. Here the stream descends from a gentle valley through a narrow cut, squeezed between two steep canyon walls. The riffle as it leaves the little meadow is perhaps sixty or eighty feet across, and easily waded. As it splashes and churns down over the rocks below, it narrows in places to twenty feet or less.

From the road it was a few minutes' walk to the meadow where we crossed the stream and followed a faint trail a half mile down the south bank. Here the trail ended at The Falls. The water tumbled down among huge boulders, then dropped over a shelf and thundered straight down some ten feet into a boiling cauldron below.

Just beside the foot of the falls a big rock the size of an automobile lay separated from the hillside by a rushing little side arm of the rapids; this gap was conveniently bridged by an old fallen tree, giving easy if cautious access to the gently sloping top of the rock. From here one could reach out with the rod tip and touch the falling water; could almost see up over the lip of the falls to the flat stretch above; and could step down knee-deep into the edge of the circular pool, onto a narrow bar of gravel which sloped off abruptly into the depths of the frothing turmoil.

Standing on this rock, it was hard to believe that the rest of the world existed. In front, rising from the far side of the falls and pool, was a sheer cliff face. Behind was a steep shale slope with a few scattered lodgepole pines. To the left was the falls itself; and to the right the seething foam coalesced again into a solid mass of green water, plunged over a narrow ledge and slid around out of sight behind the point of the hill about twenty yards away. It was like being in the bottom of a huge funnel, immersed in sound and fine mist, with only the blue sky and rim of treetops above seeming connected to the old mundane affairs outside.

There were tactical problems here. Experience had shown that the fish lay in the deepest part of the pool, against the cliff at the far side, resting before attempting the leap over the falls. Measured in ordinary mortal distances, this was a small pool. It was necessary to toss the hook just against the cliff, wait exactly long enough for it to sink to the bottom, and before the current could whisk the line out of position, give a sharp sweeping jerk. A slight miscalculation in timing or a bit too much follow-through meant a three-ounce lead missile bristling with barbs hurtling past one's head; at this point, to the snagger's companion the rock seemed awfully crowded.

The second problem was that, once hooked, the fish had more choices than the fisherman: it could stay in the kettle, or it could head down into the rapids below. There was no way to follow it, as the only exit from the rock led across the log in the opposite direction.

This was definitely a place for our heaviest gear, for the obvious strategy was to keep the fish from going downstream. If it was hooked near the head, and if it vacillated on its first attempt, it was sometimes possible to turn the fish as it headed down, and bring it back around into the whirlpool; this would tire it enough to even up the chances. But aided by that kind of moving water, a fifteen pound fish hooked amidships and determined to go downstream will go downstream regardless, and we had many a broken ninety-pound-test linen line to prove it.

The alternative to applying maximum drag on the spool with one's thumb and bracing oneself for the sickening snap (never mind the blisters) was to let the fish go down and out of sight around the bend, the line rubbing up and down against the rocky point. This only compounded the problem, for even when fully exhausted the fish couldn't possibly be hauled back up the rapids and within reach of the gaff. Finally, however, we developed a collaborative technique which was to pay off repeatedly through the years. It required three people, preferably four.

When a fish was hooked, it would usually stay almost motionless against the cliff for perhaps half a minute. It would then begin moving about, circling once or twice, and then head down over the lip of the pool. If the assailant was unable to turn the fish back into the pool, he would keep on some pressure but let the fish slide down the rapids, stopping the retreat just out of sight around the point in relatively smooth water. Meanwhile two assistants would scramble ashore and head up across the steep shale slide and downstream. One took our second rod and climbed down onto a narrow ledge next to where the hooked fish lay struggling, and prepared to try to snag it.

Because the roar of the falls made shouting necessary even for ordinary conversation from three feet away, the person below and invisible from the rock had no way to let the person attached to the fish know what was going on, so the third person was stationed high on the hill where he could see and be seen by both of the participants and could pass hand signals back and forth as required.

When everybody was ready, number two signalled to number one via number three to slack off slowly, letting the fish drift down until it was in good position. Once number two had set his hook in the fish, number one was then directed to slack off further, slowly, as the fish was brought in toward the ledge. Number four, if any, would be ready to gaff the fish – taking care to avoid impaling himself on one of the many barbs now protruding from the flapping fish. The fish was landed, carefully killed, than carried back up over the rather precarious hillside to greet its original captor.

Once I was playing the part of number four, and was getting ready to gaff a fish that my uncle had hooked and lowered around the point for Dad to snag again. I stepped down onto the crumbly ledge where Dad was standing, and just as he hooked the fish the chunk of rock I was standing on broke off and I dropped into the water. Dad hesitated to see whether my greatest hazard would be getting tangled among the lines and fish and snag hooks, or being swept off down the rapids.

I had no trouble crawling back up onto the ledge; but I was humiliated to report that I had lost our gaff in the river; and chagrined to discover that my yellow felt hat with the woven leather band that I had made the summer before had floated away and vanished. There was compensation, later, in relating to Mom how I had saved myself from the grip of the rapids by clinging to the rock and pulling myself back to safety. (I almost overplayed it; she seemed reluctant for a while to let us go fishing in the canyon.)

We always took turns snagging at the Falls, since there was only room for one rod to be wielded at a time. Twenty or thirty minutes was a fair turn, enough to get your arms and shoulders tired if you were only twelve or fourteen, and enough to discharge a little of the eager and intense anticipation that burned in each of us every time the hook disappeared into that invisible world beneath the foam. This left time for the others to reminisce about previous adventures in this spot, or simply revel in the surroundings. Then there was the rare but unforgettable moment when, without any warning, a fish as long as a man's leg would come bursting up out of the pool, its whole body frantically undulating through the air as it smacked into the solid wall of falling water and was swept back down. I never saw one actually make it to the top; but the numbers of fish that we saw spawning farther upstream suggested that jumping at the Upper Falls was all in the day's work for a salmon.

A FISH STORY

Sometimes a true story sounds so improbable that one is reluctant to tell it, because fiction would be more credible. However, a compulsive truthfulness forces me to tell of Dad's pocket knife.

We were at the Upper Falls on Yankee Fork one afternoon – Dad, Bill, Uncle Howell, and I – and had been snagging for an hour or so without hitting a fish. Not that it mattered, really. Merely being present in this place, in the magic circle of sound and mist and black towering rock and heavy green water laced with froth, was reward enough even if salmon had never existed. Memories of previous fish hooked here, and of those rare occasions when a salmon driven by its hypothalamic sense of destiny would suddenly leap into the air and slam itself into the wall of falling water a mere arm's length from our perch – these were the added dimensions that brought us again and again to this hidden place.

The sun had moved out of sight, bringing mid-afternoon shadows into the deep recess between the mountains, and a last glint of gold was lingering on the far edge of the rapids below us. Our uncle Howell was taking one final turn dropping the hook against the cliff twenty feet away and giving the quick jerk that was all the current allowed. He was just saying that maybe we should be going soon, when he hooked a fish. It was a good respectable size, about fifteen pounds or more, and made the usual sequence of a few irresolute moments deep in the central current, then the turn and dash downstream. But it was hooked near the head, and this time Howell was able to turn it back around into the pool again. If this could be done on the first rush the chances of landing it were much improved, for by the time a fish got around to make a second such attempt it had generally lost its peak of strength and vigor and thus it best chance to survive.

97

As the fish weakened and could be maneuvered a bit, Dad stepped down off the rock, knee-deep in the edge of the foamy pool where we had found the best vantage point for landing. He gaffed the fish from below, catching it near the head but carefully avoiding snatching out the snag hook with the gaff – as we had been known to do on occasion. He got a thumb in the fish's gills and his fingers under the jaw, holding the head securely and clamping the struggling body between his legs. With the situation well in hand he removed the gaff, disengaged the snag hook (lest it catch his thigh with its free points), and reached for his pocket knife. A good heavy stick applied smartly across the top of the head will generally put an end to a fish's struggle, but it was our custom to use a knife, plunging it through the relatively thin bone just at the back of the head.

With his free hand Dad opened the knife and drove the short blade to the hilt in the slippery green head. Perhaps his aim was deflected by the awkward angle of the thrust, or by a sudden movement of the fish. In any case, instead of the expected abrupt rigid tensing and fine overall quivering followed by inert limpness, the result was a heaving lunge of the fish which tore its jaw from his grasp and the knife from the other hand. The fish shot from between his legs and vanished into the foam.

We watched the surface of the swirling water, and the foot of the pool where the foam thinned and the water was again green and translucent, but we watched in vain. It seemed foolish to suppose that the fish might still have strength enough, after being gaffed in a vital area and with a pocket knife protruding from its brain, to return to its former position in the boiling current. However, the obvious thing to do was to have a go at it again, just in case. Howell was a bit tired by this time, so Dad began the rhythmic cast-sink-jerk, retrieve, cast-sink-jerk, retrieve, methodically working the space below the cliff foot by foot, then back to the upper end and cover the area again, series after series of casts along the ten-foot expanse where we knew the fish might rest. After about twenty minutes of this, abruptly and unheralded as always, cast-sink-jerk-whomp! and he was into a fish. We held our breaths as he turned the beast out of its downstream surge – more easily than usual – and brought it around by the rock and into view. The knife handle still projected from its skull like a bizarre periscope!

Howell gaffed the fish, swung it up onto the rock, and this time the knife completed its work. The salmon, though anonymous until that day and anonymously eaten, became a hero in our eyes and was posthumously enshrined in our memories and our legends as the fish that was caught and killed twice.

THE FAMILY HOLE

Near the foot of the upper canyon of Yankee Fork was the perfect spot for voyeurs. The stream came down through a narrow channel, deep and flat. The current broke against a cliff on one side, created a large eddy on the other, then spread out into a wide, gravel-bottomed shallow. This in turn broke into a rocky riffle with white water and lots of fish cover. The result was an ideal spawning shallow about fifty by seventy-five feet, sloping upstream into deep hiding water.

Some fifteen feet above, on the cliff top, was a patch of flat ground, shaded by lodgepole pines and padded with duff. Our family often brought a picnic lunch and spent several delightful hours watching chinook salmon at their most crucial endeavors.

The mating practices of these fish are polyandrous; that is, each female, while laying eggs, is attended by a more or less constant harem of males. The actual site of the egg laying is, I understand, referred to by the well informed as a "redd." We call it a bed, and I refuse to give up the habit. Besides, it is hardly credible that a free-swimming saltwater fish could be lured into a starvation journey more than a thousand miles up a freshwater stream to its certain death, by the prospect of making love in a "redd."

This particular hole was of a size to be taken over by one female and her male entourage. Around the first of July we would start watching for signs of occupancy. Even if the fish were in hiding when we came by, the beginnings of the work were obvious. The female's labors would disturb the gravel, turning some bottom-up. Since the stream bed generally is coated with a thin organic film, disturbance of this nature left an easily identified light spot. This spot would gradually grow, until it was six to ten feet wide and fifteen to twenty feet long. As she loosened the gravel the current would

100

carry it downstream a bit, so that the final result was an oval area scooped out about a foot below the stream bed at the upper end, and heaped up a bit at the lower end. The female would start at the lower end of the bed, turn over onto her side, and slowly flap her way to the upper end, loosening and moving the gravel with her head, tail and belly as she went. The currently privileged male would follow closely, perhaps slightly to one side, performing the same ecstatic dance. They would then let the current drift them back over the bed, where they would rest a few minutes. Occasionally the female would whirl and make what seemed to be an attack on following trout. These we could see behind her, in a rough line graded according to size, waiting for eggs to drop. She scattered them only momentarily, after which the trout train quickly reformed.

The female stolidly carried on this ritual, completely indifferent to the presence or absence of the males. She never interfered with the lively theatrics by which they allocated turns. It was, however, the antics of the males that drew us to the cliff-top for hilarious picnics. On a good day there might be four or five, ranging in size from twenty pounds down to two. For the males, timing was everything. The largest, a great sleek, hooknosed beast, his sides turned dark red in his dotage, could only be displaced by guile; force was of no avail. One of the others would slip up from the riffle below and assume a strategic spot for the next spawning pass. The large male, resting after his exertions, would become aware of this insolence and, whirling, drive the intruder down into the fast water below. The coast was now clear for a third male to scoot up and join the female. The master would return from his chase to discover the new invader, and furiously repel him, but too late. Thus the advantages of size and strength could be neutralized, and the pro-creative powers of even the smallest be not wasted.

In the endless variations of this game, we regularly rooted for the little males. We named them all, tried to anticipate their strategy, cheered them on. One tiny male that couldn't have exceeded eighteen inches in length slipped up beside the master of the day, grabbed his right pectoral fin and backed water for all he was worth. The big one turned, lost sight of his prey, and shot downstream in pursuit of nothing, while the little one successfully achieved his moment.

Later on, when my biology teachers told me I should never anthropomorphize nature, I just figured they had never spent an afternoon at the Family Hole.

A footnote: When our youngest son was about eight, he asked me one day where babies come from. Given that he was a fisherman and I needed time to think, I started by launching on some version of the above description. He interrupted. "Wait a minute, Dad. I want to go and turn up the radio. There's some really sad music that would go great with this."

Where did I go wrong?

A DAY IN THE LIFE

"Isn't life beautiful
Isn't life gay
Isn't life the perfect thing
To pass the time away"
Mason Williams song

In the summers, whenever we were in the mountains, fishing was the primary activity. It was a rare day that didn't start with fishing – usually for salmon – at daylight. After the morning fishing and breakfast, however, there were many options. There was firewood to gather and cut. There was water to carry, a few hundred yards in a ten-gallon cream can (not filled all the way up and still it was quite a struggle, but at least it was all down hill). Occasionally a new garbage pit needed to be dug. Often there was a salmon to be skinned and filleted. Sometimes Bill and I went swimming (wading and splashing mostly). There were sucker minnows and other bait to be caught in a length of window screen nailed to a stick at each end, spread out across the current and held by one person while another chased the minnows down into the net. Maybe once every week or two we took all our dirty clothes to the Hot Spring, with soap and washboard, and wallowed in the steamy and sulphurous bathhouse.

Then there were infinite ad hoc possibilities. Once (I blush to relate) I confirmed reports that a frog, carefully inflated via the anus by blowing through a straw, cannot readily stay submerged; and a large sucker, caught and encumbered by a wooden float tied to his tail with a two-foot piece of string, was not as encumbered as I had thought and to my guilty dismay disappeared promptly and permanently in the quiet pond below the dam, float and all.

Afternoons were varied. When we were in the guiding business and had a fishing party who hadn't yet caught their fish, of course this took precedence over all else. If not, sometimes we did family things – meaning Mom went along. Perhaps a picnic lunch – and some trout fishing. Maybe a trip down river, exploring less familiar territory toward Clayton. A trip to someplace we had never been before, or to some old favorite place. Usually some fishing was included, and Mom sewed, read, wrote, or walked around and explored. On such a day we would likely return after dark, singing or making outlandish puns, or just riding in silence, subdued by delicious fatigue and the magically peaceful surroundings.

The gentle hiss of the gasoline lantern presided over the evening activities. The fishing rods were stood on the ground against the front of the house or, in bad weather or when there were a lot of tourists around, hung on wire hooks high on the living room wall. The fish were put away – trout in a wet bag on the side of the house where the rising sun wouldn't reach them or, if they weren't going to be eaten for breakfast, in the cooler down in the old tunnel; a salmon would be hung on a spike by the front door, for advertising.

The wood box would be refilled from the stack at the back of the house. Meanwhile Mom would have a fire going and someone would set the table.

There's something cosmically satisfying about coming home after a long day of hiking, working, or wading and fishing; replacing the wet cold socks and shoes with dry ones; and gathering with the family in that little island of light, listening to the murmur of the river while eating a hot but simple meal. Supper might be warmed-over fish chowder, or corn meal mush, or "slum gullion" (Mom's version was a mixture of rice or macaroni with tomatoes, and either hamburger or bacon); and canned fruit.

Afterward Bill or I – sometimes – would help Mom do the dishes, if she had kept the fire going to heat the water.

Finally, when the oilcloth-covered table had been cleared off and the lantern replaced in its center, we could lay out our evening's chores.

On a typical evening Mom might be mending, or writing a letter. Bill would be cutting strips of sheet lead for sinkers, and tying up some leaders to replace those lost to rocks and logs of the aquatic underworld. Dad would sharpen some bait hooks and snag hooks, and replace a guide on a rod or re-wrap the butt section with chalk line and secure a loosened reel seat. I would have collected the bolt of red mosquito-netting, the quart jar of preserved salmon eggs, and assorted scraps of grocery twine, and slid onto the bench between the table and the wall to prepare for the next morning's fishing. (It was always distressing, and a bit of a disgrace, to run out of baits and have to stop fishing to tie some up during the morning.)

If the salmon gear was all in order, perhaps we would play rummy, or tie a few flies, or clean and oil a box of trout lures (mostly Colorado spinners), or sharpen a pocket knife. This was also a time for whittling; I spent countless hours of my youth (and my middle age) whittling chains, balls in cages, and assorted variations and embellishments of these themes.

Soon enough it was already late; the gasoline was low and the lantern would begin to fade; myriad moths, gnats, crane flies, and other unfortunate denizens of the night, their navigational reflexes deluded by this siren false-moon, ended their helical errands as a sad circle of quick-fried crumbs about the base of the lamp (sometimes, in final revenge, flying through the lantern's fragile mantle). With thoughts of a four or five o'clock appointment with tomorrow's dawn, we set the alarm and crawled into bed. The river crooned its unending song, a night breeze whispered accompaniment in the fir tree by the back porch, and a mouse in the attic on some earnest business pattered across the ceiling. Thus turned on its axis another of the early days of our being and becoming.

IN PRAISE OF USELESS ACTION

From time to time – perhaps in deference to our mother – instead of spending the morning fishing we would simply go for a drive, see some sights. Mom would fix a picnic lunch (and we might have some fishing gear along, just in case).

On one such a day in midsummer, the sky crystal clear and the air pleasantly warm and fragrant of pine and sage, we drove down river toward no hard destination. Four miles below Sunbeam we crossed the bridge at Robinson's Bar and continued on down the east side. At one place, from the road high above the river you could look down a stretch of canyon for what appeared to be many miles, with shadowed ravines and small valleys feeding their mysterious secrets into the main channel. Our parents were chatting about some bit of business or politics and Bill and I were taking turns holding a little home-made windmill out the window.

Suddenly Mom gave a gasping cry. I looked up in time to see her clutch at her neck or chest and she said, "I hurt!"

Dad stopped the car abruptly in the middle of the road (there was no other place to stop). All three of us leaned toward Mom, hovering, not knowing what was happening. She looked frightened, fists still clenched against her bosom. Dad reached and touched her shoulder, but nothing changed; she didn't speak.

"I'll get you some water!" Dad said. He fumbled in the picnic box, found a white enameled cup, looked at her once more, and plunged over the shoulder of the road toward the river. He leaped, strode, slid, and clattered down the steep shale slope, down a hundred feet or so to the bottom. He scooped up a cup of water and started back up toward the car. Scrambling and clawing, he climbed up and slid back, fell at least twice, all the while holding the cup, and made gradual headway. A couple of times I glanced at Mom – she seemed to be improving – but I worried more now about Dad. At last he reached the edge of the road, crawled on his knees to the car's running board, stretched his arm out to hand the cup (still, incredibly, half full of water) to Mom, then collapsed gasping against the wheel of the car.

Mom's sudden attack of pain had quit. In ten minutes Dad had recovered enough to drive on. We had a nice picnic lunch, and completed our excursion uneventfully. But a half-century later I can still feel deep inside of me a reprise of that scene: my father racing, at considerable peril to life and limb, to deliver to his wife a half cup of water because *he didn't know anything better to do,* and because *something had to be done.*

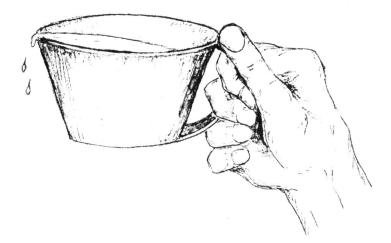

Examples occur all the time where futile actions, useless gestures are absolutely required: A mother picks up her dead child and holds him tightly against her. A man holding his neighbor's garden hose sprinkles the dying embers of the remains of his own house. A funeral ceremony, however you want to do it.

Years ago, as an Emergency Department physician I was on duty when the patient being rushed in by ambulance was Marty, one of our own ER nurses, a close member of our professional family, shot in the chest by a drunken boyfriend.

We worked on her for an hour, four doctors and a lot of nurses and technicians – CPR, tracheal intubation, heart monitor, multiple IV's, blood transfusions, finally opening her chest and massaging her naked heart – even though we knew after the first couple of minutes that she was dead beyond rescue. We all had to go through these motions before any of us was ready to say, "Stop".

At last we were able to lay down our tools, brush the tears, and concede defeat Suddenly I thought of Dad, desperate on the crumbling hillside, holding out the cup.

POLE CREEK

As the Salmon River in its infancy reaches the foot of Galena Mountain and begins its wandering toward adolescence in the valley floor, it is joined by Pole Creek. This modest little stream is in a few places too wide to jump across but nowhere is it too much to wade across in four steps. The sign where it crosses under the main road was one of the landmarks we always noted, but only once, as I remember, did we ever stop there.

We heard a rumor that, unimpressive as the stream appeared, it contained some decent bull trout, or Dolly Varden (*Salvelinus malma*), a type of charr which were fairly abundant in the river below. One day, after our salmon fishing urges had been temporarily assuaged, we decided to give it a try. Taking a picnic lunch, we left in mid-morning on the forty-mile trip to Pole Creek. We found a shady place to park between willows and sagebrush fifty yards off the highway, left Mom in charge of the broader aspects of exploring, and each chose a section of stream.

Bill and I each caught a half-dozen or so, some cutthroats and some bull trout in the seven- to nine-inch category, gratifying enough for a stream this size, and I had headed upstream to see how Dad was doing when I heard his distant shout. Hurrying in that direction I was impeded by dense willows and it was some minutes before I broke through into clear meadow again. There Dad met me, sopping wet and carrying a fish that hung to his knees.

He had been calling, it seemed, simply to share with us his astonishment at the improbable event: a three-pound bull trout, which, with its long, slinky shape, meant some two feet of length. He had hooked it in a deep spot beneath an undercut bank, on a size 16 hook with a single salmon egg. It had immediately headed downstream. As Dad started to follow, it changed its mind and, plunging almost between his legs, rushed upstream. Pole Creek is closely set about with willows in many places, so that any consistent traffic is limited to the stream itself; thus went the fish, with Dad in frantic pursuit, sometimes crawling almost on his belly in midstream with his rod thrust straight out in front of him to get under the tangled brush. Around bends and through potholes and riffles, some hundred yards the fish led him before it was too tired to flee further.

Dad hadn't removed the hook from the fish's mouth, because he wanted to demonstrate to us how precarious the situation had been: the little gold hook, engaged in the edge of the huge upper jaw, was straightened out to a mere ninety-degree bend by the tension on the four-pound test leader, but had held on just long enough.

After lunch we tried another stretch of stream, but the hot midriff of the day is often not the most productive for trout fishing, and so it proved. We dressed our fish and headed back, in time to make the evening salmon fishing at The Ledge.

For some reason we never returned to Pole Creek – perhaps for fear of diluting out the memories of a legendary event.

ALL-PURPOSE HUNTING DOG

Rex came into our lives as a tiny puppy, riding inside the front of Uncle Bud's shirt, when I was about ten or eleven. He remained part of our family for many years.

I recall that he was identified from the beginning as "five-eighths English pointer". This mathematical nicety was never explained to my satisfaction, but his shape didn't miss that of the customary pointer by very much, and experiences over the years did reveal traces of the pointer's instinctive tendencies. He was devoid of any effective training, as what very little Dad knew about how to train a bird dog was more than cancelled by his being a family dog subjected to a chaotic mix of instructions and rewards for he knew not what, and punishments geared more to our moods than to any technique or philosophy of training. Not that he didn't get experience; Dad hunted pheasants and ducks, and Rex went along and enjoyed every minute. I well remember seeing a jack rabbit, Rex, and Dad in train, separated each by about fifty yards, galloping at full throttle through the sagebrush toward the horizon; the rabbit was silent, Rex was yelping excitedly, and Dad was brandishing his shotgun and shouting, "Rex! Rex! Confound you, come back here." Rex was, in fact, able to smell out a pheasant in weeds or stubble, and was occasionally actually seen pointing in classic style for a fraction of a second – before he rushed in and flushed the bird just out of range of the hunters.

When we went fishing, Rex often went along. He had lots of opportunity to watch and learn – and we were sometimes surprised to find that he had done just that.

One day on Marsh Creek, as we were walking back up the path by the stream toward camp, we noticed that Rex was acting strangely. In fact, he was standing and holding the best point I had ever seen him perform, with one front foot lifted and motionless, staring out toward the middle of the river; he then walked slowly up the bank a few steps and repeated the point. We looked out into the shallow riffle and, to our astonishment, saw a large salmon, its dorsal fin just above the surface, moving up and then out of sight in deeper water.

Some years later Rex was still learning the rules of the game. Bill and I were fishing for salmon from The Ledge at Sunbeam Dam, and someone whom we didn't know was fishing for trout from the rocks below. He had caught several trout, and had scooped out a little hollow in the gravel beach, a couple of feet in diameter, which filled up with water and made a cool place in which to keep his fish protected from the heat of the sun. Suddenly we heard a voice below, and saw that Rex had carefully lifted the fellow's five or six fish out of the little pool and laid them in a pile on the sand.

We went down, put the fish back in the water, scolded Rex (who seemed a bit puzzled), apologized to the stranger, and went back to our fishing.

A half hour later one of us caught a salmon, about a twelve-pounder as I remember. We dressed it and laid it in the shade of some rocks while going back to fish some more. Shortly I heard another shout, this time from Bill, and looked down just in time to see Rex dragging the salmon down the bank and into the water; he nosed it out into the current, and stood watching it drift slowly away. Rushing frantically down from The Ledge and into the edge of the river, I saw the fish roll over out of reach and disappear.

Poor Rex! Was his people's objective to get the fish out of the water, or back into the water? No matter how he tried, he just couldn't seem to get it right, could never satisfy us. Fishing is just too complicated for a five-eighths dog.

THE UNEXPECTED GRAVITY OF AN EXPERIMENT

Among Llew Clawson's effects when he died was an old book on mineralogy. Looking through it I found instructions for making a simple device for measuring the specific gravity of mineral samples or other objects (that is, their density compared with that of water).

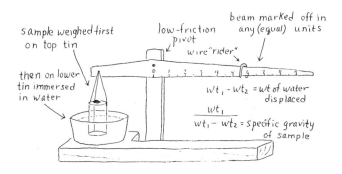

It was a mere matter of a couple of hours to fabricate the machine out of scraps of materials easily available (pieces of an orange crate, a small nail, a piece of wire, a bit of thread, and the bottoms cut from a couple of tin cans). I tried it on several objects that came to hand, and was delighted and amazed to find my results checking out very closely with the table in the back of the book: a piece of quartz from the back yard, 2.6; a shingle nail, 7.5; a dime (they were silver in those days), 10.5; a small lead sinker, 11.3; some mercury (which we happened to have on hand for our gold panning project), 13.6; and Mom's gold wedding band, 19.2.

Looking for more samples to try, I approached Aunt Maurine, who with Uncle Howell was visiting us. She had been showing her platinum wedding ring, of which she and Uncle Howell were rather proud. A bit reluctantly she removed it from her finger and watched me fiddling with my toy, anxious to have the ring back on her hand again.

But there was some little trouble. I checked and rechecked my reading on the scale, checked for air bubbles trapped under the can lid – everything seemed all right, and testing again a sample of iron confirmed that the gadget was still working properly.

Platinum is the heaviest of the natural metals, but the specific gravity of her ring, instead of the value given in the book, 21.0, was less than that by nearly fifteen percent; yet every other object I had tested had been within five percent of the listed values.

At first she dismissed my concern; a crude toy, thrown together and appearing so odd, was hardly expected to be very accurate. But I persisted, and showed her my other figures from a half-dozen other substances with consistently repeatable results. Finally she began to frown. Then she became very silent, looked at the ring for a couple of minutes, and disappeared. I heard her in earnest conversation with Uncle Howell behind the closed door of the bedroom, and their voices gradually rose in volume and in pitch.

A few minutes later Mom came out to the porch and firmly suggested that my machine and I get lost, and that I refrain from stirring up trouble in the family in the future. Fragments of talk of alloys to make the platinum hard enough to wear well reached my ears, but I knew naught of metallurgy and merely slunk away.

A GOOD DAY AND BAD AT THE THREE FALLS

The Three Falls was perhaps the second best place on Yankee Fork for blind snagging. It was a quarter mile or so below the Upper Falls, that spectacular theater of team snagging and broken lines, and was a less breath-taking place but fine nevertheless. Here, in the midst of the rapids, the stream abruptly dropped some four feet over a broad ledge. Most of the water was channelled between large boulders into a roaring fall and a frothy pool, which tailed out quickly into a gentle riffle and then more rapids. As you stood thigh-deep in this riffle and faced the fall, at your left were two minor diversions of the current that dashed merrily over the same ledge and made their separate ways through the rocks to rejoin the main stream. By standing on a stone slab just beside the pool you could cast up and across and sweep the hook into deep water where the fish were wont to lie.

I had become reasonably adept at the various aspects of salmon fishing, and when Dad was serving as guide to a party of fishermen, Bill or I regularly accompanied him as assistants and participants in the job. The deal was that for five dollars we would guarantee that the party had a fish to take home or no pay, and that we would try to help them catch one themselves.

We were fishing the Three Falls; Dad was snagging and showing the customer how, while I stood by with the gaff. Suddenly Dad hooked a good big fish, probably twenty pounds, and I quickly waded out into position in the riffle below. The salmon gave a short rush toward the falls and hung there in deeper water for a few moments; then, jumping clear of the water and somersaulting once, he churned down toward me. I gaffed him all right, just behind the head, and with the fish thrashing back and forth but suspended safely by the gaff I waded toward the shore some eight feet away. Half way there the fish's movement threw the weighted snag hook from his side, and at the same instant my foot slipped off a rock. I didn't fall, but in trying to right myself I let the gaff turn and drop a few inches, and the fish splashed into the water between my legs. In vain I lashed at the hole in the water as he vanished.

The entire act had scarcely spanned a minute, and the customer, having just seen his first live salmon, stood open-mouthed. Dad said nothing at first, then made some remark intended to be consoling and encouraging to both me and our guest. Having gotten the idea in a hurry, the man tried his hand at snagging. I stood in the tail of the foam, trying to let the water that was pulling at my knees wash away my humiliation. I only hoped that he would hook one so that I could redeem myself.

I had not long to wait. Within five minutes he was attached to a fish, and a big one – definitely bigger than the first, a stout male with red sides. I braced myself as he came bearing down toward me angling off to the right.

A big fish hooked near the tail and aided by the current hardly seems to be impeded much by a mere man connected to him by a line, and this fish was moving fast; I shouldn't have tried to take him from there, but I did. The gaff sank home, but too far back near the middle of the fish. I lifted him from the water, a glorious beast with his huge mouth wide open, the hooked nose pointing to the sky and the hot afternoon sun flashing from his belly. Then the fisherman unexpectedly heaved back on the rod; the fish's broad tail swung sharply upward, pivoting him on the gaff and at the same time flipping the snaghook free. To my horror the weight was lifted from the gaff and the fish continued his curving trajectory to plunge back into the pool.

I was too old to cry, but inside I wept bitter tears. This time a palpable tension filled the air, and the curses, though muted, were plainly for me. I retired to the rock, and someone firmly relieved me of the gaff.

I'm not quite clear on what followed -- whether the guest hooked another or whether Dad hooked it for him and handed him the rod. It was a smaller fish, not nearly so grand as the others. Dad gaffed it and firmly clutched its jaw with his other hand while he brought it ashore. The guarantee was fulfilled, and the man was quite gracious about the whole thing (he also took home another fish that we had on hand as well). Dad passed it off, as best he could, as just of those unlucky breaks. But it took more than one fish successfully landed to restore fully my confidence in my place as a member of the team.

HARROD ENKING

The year I was in the sixth grade we moved to Fairfield, Idaho, Dad became principal-teacher-coach of Camas County High School, and Harrod Enking came into our lives. We had known him before, as a family friend and a student of Mom's at Gooding College; but now he came as a teacher in the high school – one of the five, including Dad.

Harrod was tall, slender, and quite handsome. He was meticulous in various ways but especially in his speech – not in a contrived way, but he just talked well, clearly and deliberately. My remembering also has him gentle, courtly, kind, and honorable; but his greatest contribution to our household was his sense of humor in the spoken word. Though there was plenty of laughter around our house before, the era of really continuous fun with the language – the lived understanding that words are both tools and toys – began with Harrod, and thereafter a five-minute conversation without a pun or two was reckoned dull.

He seemed very young at the time – his first teaching job, and just out of college – and at first he was a little shy and deferential toward our parents; but he fell quickly enough into a solid place in the family dynamics, like some sort of uncle to Bill and me, and through most of those years was an integral part of the adult world around me. He took a job elsewhere before I got into high school so I never had him for a teacher – not formally, that is. Nevertheless he was one of my important linguistic role models. He visited often over the next ten years and became one of our favorite fishing companions, until at last the Air Force carried him out of our domain.

Puns come and go (fortunately!) and I can remember only one actual example of Merrill-Enking humor, an outrageous conversation as we were all in the car, riding through a sloppy night in the spring mud season. We were splashing through water-filled potholes and slithering a bit here and there. Windshield washers had not yet been invented, and the wipers alone merely scraped the worst of it off to the sides. The conversation, through the haze of forty-some years, comes back to me something like this:

Harrod: "I say, that windshield is rather opaque."

Dad: "Yes, quite opaque" (rolling the window down to see where we were going).

Harrod: "Even the side window is a little opaque -- in fact, the whole "O'Paque" family is with us, bless their Irish hearts!"

With tears of laughter, as Harrod got out to wipe the glass, we all began the scramble for naming more of the "O'Paque" clan: Very, Somewhat, Scarcely, Unduly, and on and on. Even days later, he who could add a new and suitably lyrical adverb-turned-noun to the "O'Paque" family tree would be applauded.

Harrod's father had been dead for many years, but I met his mother, Myrtle Enking (who later became Idaho State Treasurer). I came to know this dear lady as the embodiment of the real meaning of "gentlewoman," and I could readily see how Harrod – an only child – had come by the charming nature which lent such sparkle to our fishing and our living.

THE LEGEND OF CASTO

Some ten miles north of Sunbeam Dam the Yankee Fork valley contained the biodegraded remnants of two mining towns, Custer and Bonanza. Halfway between them, Jordan Creek (pronounced "Jer-den") came down from the west. A single-track road followed Jordan Creek to and beyond the ghost town of Sunbeam. Past Sunbeam it climbed in marvelously sharp switchbacks up and over a high ridge and descended into the valley of Loon Creek on the other side. There it passed a small ranch and ended at a most magic spot.

Cap Sebree had made the magic for us with a tale I have never been able to confirm entirely, though hearsay years later lent support. The tale, told to Ted and me by Cap:

Where the Loon Creek road ended in 1936, there once stood a town called Casto. (This at least is borne out by a U.S. government map dated 1890, though by no other I have seen.) Casto was a placer mining town, populated entirely by men. About a thousand of these were Caucasian miners, and five hundred were Chinese. The Chinese had spread to such places all over the West, when the great undertakings such as the Central Pacific and Canadian Pacific railroads were completed and they were left to their own devices. Here they did the menial work of the town, and when placer ground was worked out to the point of yielding less than four dollars a day, it was turned over to them. The gold the Chinese earned by washing socks and gravel, they scrupulously saved, or so the whites assumed.

The day came when all the gravel bars were yielding less than four dollars a day, and the miners decided to abandon the town and seek their fortunes elsewhere. Considering it immoral to leave a part of the golden produce of the stream in the hands of the heathen Chinese, they roughly disguised themselves as Indians and massacred the whole Chinese population, took their belongings, burned the town, and departed.

Years later we mentioned these events to an elderly family friend in Boise. She was familiar with the story, and told us that a survivor, a man who saved himself by lying weighted with rocks on the stream bottom and breathing through a reed, was then still living in Boise. We never tried to find him, but our mother saw his obituary, including the Casto story, in a newspaper.

We drove one day to the presumed site of Casto. From that trip three perfect memory images remain to me. The first is of the town of Sunbeam, population on the day of our visit, one. The man emerged from the only inhabited shack, and pointed out some of the features of the town. The cabins and remnants of business buildings were on the north side of the creek, near the bottom of the valley. Well up the hillside to the south was the mill, still mostly intact structurally though largely stripped of its machinery. Remaining, however, was the tramway which had carried the gold ore down from the Sunbeam Mine. A huge flanged bull-wheel some twelve feet across was set flush to a cement platform. From a tower high on the mountain across the valley to the north, so far away as to be barely visible, a doubled cable swooped in one vast span, to loop around this mighty pulley; beyond the tower the cable disappeared in the direction of the mine. Spaced along the cable were the ore buckets, looking from the great distance like soup ladles hanging by their handles. It seemed an awesome incongruity, this mechanical behemoth of such enormous sophistication and power, casting its shadow on the scattering of rude log cabins and false-fronted frame buildings hundreds of feet below. How did that great steel rope, perhaps a mile or more of it, get there? It must have come a hundred miles or so from the rail's end at Ketchum, presumably by mule train. It seems an undertaking in the same league with the Inca hauling building stones to Cuzco. And there it hung, one day to come down without warning, smashing to final splinters the greyed remnants of the town.

The second of my memories of the trip to Casto is of the top of the ridge separating Jordan Creek drainage from that of Loon Creek. We stopped for a bit to look and throw stones. When we returned to the car for the equally hair-raising trip down to Loon Creek, my father, in a rare burst of vulgarity, remarked, "First place I've ever been where I could pee a mile in either direction." Water divides have always evoked special feelings in me. Perhaps it was Dad's example which led me, years later, to stop at South Pass in the Wyoming Rockies to urinate at the exact crest, in the hope that some of my molecules might reach the Pacific and some the Gulf of Mexico.

The third memory is of the town site of Casto itself. Cap had described it as it had been when alive. We had to recognize its corpse, and did. The fire must have been thorough, leaving no sign of a building. Where the hill broke steeply from the valley floor, the door-frame logs of a small dugout remained. All other signs of a settlement of 1500 people were concealed in the short meadow grass. Along the stream, however, tracks of the mining abounded. Gravel was piled in ways foreign to stream runoff. A wooden flume, empty now, still clung to the face of a cliff, above the reach of spring floods. It had once delivered water to the miners' sluice boxes and rockers.

While Dad went fishing, Ted and Mom and I searched for proof of Cap's grisly tale of slaughter. Our findings, though inadequate perhaps for history, were quite enough to satisfy our imaginings. Cap had told us that the whites had lived on a raised bench, and the Chinese on the lower flat near the river. As I recall, our adolescent thirst for vicarious blood concentrated our search on the lower flat where the massacre presumably happened. There we found unmistakable foundation stones for small cabins, a few rifle cartridge cases, and nothing else. I think we expected to find skulls and leg bones and little carved figures of the Buddha inside those foundations, but a handful of rifle cartridges was, after all, enough.

THE BLINDEST OF BLIND SNAGGING

During the height of the salmon run, even in those days, there was a lot of competition for some of the fishing holes, and of all the holes in the river, fishing was by far the heaviest at The Ledge. This platform of rock, about fifteen feet above the water, overlooked the double eddy below the blown-out end of the dam and was the best all-around fishing spot on the river. There was room for three people at a time to bait-fish for salmon if they were good friends and pretty good at handling the line and rod, and two people if they were strangers – or one person if he was aggressive and clumsy. Snagging, however, was rather treacherous for more than one, even for experts, and any spectators generally kept well back out of the way and kept a sharp lookout for an ill-timed sweep of the rod that would bring the weighted treble hook shooting out of the water to smack against the cliff by one's head.

It followed, then, that competition for first chance at The Ledge became keen at times. We had the advantage over the rest of the world, since we lived in the little old watchman's house at the edge of the river, only a couple of hundred yards from The Ledge, and had merely to crawl out of bed before daylight, pull on our pants and boots and a good warm sweat shirt, grab the rod standing beside the door, and trot down over the rocks and climb up into the cherished place. However, there was a time when we found ourselves having to get up earlier and earlier to get to the spot before the first comers, and then wait in the chill night's end until we could see the line well enough to fish. Some hardy souls even came and stayed all night, driving their car down past the house on the rocky path and trying (without much success) to shine the headlights on the water so they could fish.

We didn't wish to be greedy, and generally in such a case we would feel that anybody who wanted to fish there that badly should probably have a chance to do so. However, Bill and I were staying there alone for several weeks one summer, and had no transportation of our own, so we were pretty limited in where we could fish. We were hiring out as salmon fishing guides, and when we had a party to take fishing they took us with them. But as guides, we guaranteed that the customer would at least have a fish to take home, even if we couldn't guarantee that he would catch one himself; therefore it was always good to have a fish on hand in case of such emergency.

One time, when the fishing pressure had been on, we had a party engaged for the following morning and had not caught a fish for several days. The Ledge had been occupied all day, and we were getting a bit worried about our guarantee, so we decided for once to try it at night. The people with the lanterns, car lights, and lots of persistence came again at dusk and looked ready to stay forever.

Bill and I set the alarm for two in the morning, and dragged ourselves out to see what was happening. Sure enough, there was a lantern visible on The Ledge, but just about then the pair of determined fishermen adjourned to their car and their fire for a cup of coffee and to get warm. We strolled down and greeted them, learned that they hadn't caught anything, and felt our way over and up and took the place on The Ledge.

Snagging here required a moderately long cast, rather precise control of the tension on the line as the hook sank and was carried around the center of the eddy on the far side, and then accurate timing of the jerks and slacking off to get two good swings of the rod without bringing the hook flying up at our faces.

It was a black, moonless night, but we had a flashlight, and found that we could get by quite well if one held the light and tried to shine it on the spot where the hook splashed into the water; this, along with the feel, gave the really necessary information for the maneuver that was to follow.

We had snagged about twenty minutes, taking turns holding the light, when I hooked a fish. The darkness suddenly seemed several shades darker as we tried in vain to see where the fish was or in which direction the line was pointing; the feel and bend in the rod gave distressingly inadequate data. As was the usual practice, Bill ran down over the rocks with the gaff (and the light) while by memory and feel I let the rod lead me across the point and down the steep remains of the old fish ladder to get down to water level. Bill waded out into the edge of the current, gaff in one hand and flashlight in the other, trying to see where the line was and waiting for the fish to be let down to him. Suddenly he felt the line taut across his face as the fish, whose location I could only roughly guess, thrashed down past him. Bill staggered out onto the bank and raced farther down, calling to me to try to check the fish where it was. Finally we were able to see it as it came to the surface and churned up a white circle of froth. Slithering and stumbling, Bill swung the gaff at the victim, a good fifteen pounder, but struck the line instead and the hook was knocked free. Just as Bill loosed an anguished cry, the confused fish turned and beached itself among the rocks. In the dancing circle of feeble light, we threw ourselves on top of the fish and dissolved in gales of laughter and mutual congratulations.

Neither Bill nor I is the boastful type, but as we casually strolled back with our fish past the coffee drinkers (who offered no comment) I fear that even the heavy darkness could not conceal our broad grins. We were back between the blankets a scant three quarters of an hour after leaving the house.

THE PRIZE FISH

One lazy lunchtime in mid-July Bill and I pondered on how to spend the afternoon. It was during the month or so when the parents, with some misgivings, had left us in charge of the house at Sunbeam Dam and had gone back to Fairfield to tend to some business. We had enough for food staples for a month, if it was spent prudently and supplemented by fish; the necessary fishing equipment; the possibility of inducing tourists to engage us as fishing guides; and surroundings that we loved. It was the first time we had ever been there alone. It was a great time.

We had no fish on hand, and it was prudent to have a salmon on hand at all times, so that if we had the good fortune to be hired by a fishing party and then the bad luck not to catch a fish, they would still have a fish to take home and we could keep the five-dollar fee. We had no transportation but our feet, so unless we were with a fishing party and their car, our salmon fishing range was sharply limited.

We discussed whether to "take the afternoon off" and fish down the river for trout or to snag a while at The Ledge. The blind snagging was work, and sometimes tedious for the one watching and waiting with the gaff. The rhythm — cast, let it sink, the two sharp jerks with a pause between, then reel in and repeat, over and over and over – after an hour or two this could become a bit tiring; yet each cast and each movement was driven by past occasions sharply remembered in the muscles of hands and shoulders and thighs, memories of the sudden unpredicted contact with a fish, the sudden shift of balance to keep from falling off the rock, the adjustment of thumb pressure on the reel, the piece of wood from Asia bent full against the piece of meat from the Pacific here in their strange mountain rendezvous.

We decided on snagging, and the next three or four hours saw us, shirtless under the hot sun, squinting through the reflections at each invisible cubic yard catalogued in our mind's eye, methodically combing that aquatic space for the loitering fish.

Bill hooked one, but it threw the hook on its first rush across the pool. After another half hour I hooked one. Its first astonished sprint was directly away and downstream into the far side of the heavy current. I couldn't turn it before it passed the end of the island below the pool and was beyond retrieval; it broke the line and was gone.

Another hour. One of us went to the house and brought drinking water. Then Bill hooked another, a big fish. This time it chose to stay in the deep water of the channel, tiring itself fairly fast against the combined forces of the river and the line. I was in place, knee deep in the near channel below the point, as the fish struggled on the surface and came down to be landed. It was too deep to see just where the hook was

128

in the fish as it drove past me; I swung the gaff – and neatly extracted the hook, coming up with the line around the gaff as the fish vanished.

This sort of thing happened to us occasionally, and Bill was understanding, but I felt guilty and embarrassed. We went back to work, taking turns, fifteen or twenty minutes at a stretch.

The sun sets early there in the canyon, sliding behind the mountains across and upriver. The big eddy on the far side was already in shadow, the reflections from the heavy central current glinting in blinding contrast. The first faint coolness of evening was in the breeze coming down through the cut when the end of my swing with the rod met a fish, and the old reflex responses and rush of adrenalin were there on cue. The solid resistance; feeling out the unseen thing at the end of the line; setting the hook a second time, just to be sure, for it didn't move much at first, then headed right up the center of the current and over to the far side, moving deliberately and with confidence. It took one quick run to the eddy in the shadow, jumped clear of the water once, then sounded and came back toward us in the heavy current again. We had seen that it was a big male – a really big one. Bill was on the rock point, waiting with the gaff to see what the fish would decide.

It took a turn close in under the edge of the cliff beneath our feet, moving slowly but still in complete control. I was pretty sure by now that it wouldn't have the strength to get clear across to the far side of the island and beyond – its only sure route of escape; anywhere else it might go I could still keep within a line's length and follow if necessary.

The fish played out its hand in the edge of the current, surfaced once more in the upper end of the eddy by the cliff, then started downstream, and Bill quickly took his position in the edge of the riffle. I wasn't really able to check the fish as it came even with him, and he had to lunge aside out of its way as it came within reach, but he took it just behind the head and, letting the gaff move with the flailing of the fish so it wouldn't pry loose, he waded ashore. Within seconds we were both kneeling astride the fish, a hand in the gills, while the knife was opened and the fatal cerebral wound delivered.

The fish quivered and lay still. I quivered and stood up.

"Look at the size of it!" we said. "How much do you think it weighs?"

"It must be over twenty-five pounds," we replied.

"I wonder if we should weigh it in for the contest."

This year, for the first time, Howard Davis had put up a notice that an ocean-type split-bamboo rod, with reel and line, would be given away at the sunbeam store for the biggest salmon caught by the first of August. As yet, none of our fish had been of competition size.

We debated, while we dressed the fish, as to what the prize winner might have to weigh. We knew that in the ocean chinooks of sixty pounds and more were not too uncommon, but they lose up to a third of their weight on the 1,000-mile foodless trip up to our domain. I recalled seeing one gigantic fish that someone had brought to the store several years before that was reported to be forty-seven pounds, and it had always remained in my mental frame of reference as the outside limit for hopes and fantasies. Dad had once caught one – the biggest of all in our own experience – which, after dressing and a couple of days of travelling, still went twenty-nine pounds. The usual range for our biggest ones seemed to stop quite abruptly at about twenty-four or twenty-five pounds.

We struggled up the hill to the store with the fish and asked Dodger Davis to weigh it for us, murmuring something about the contest.

"But to count for the contest," Dodger said, "it has to be weighed before it's dressed, or you won't get credit for its full weight."

130

Dismay! This rule had not occurred to us. The pointer stopped at twenty-five and a half; dressed or undressed, it certainly was a record for me, and was the largest contest entry yet checked in. The suggestion that we go and bring up the missing viscera to be weighed was of no help; as was our custom, we had pitched these parts far out into the river.

We all agreed that the gills, heart, liver (always large in a salmon, and often saved for breakfast), the two large testes, the blood-like mass of kidney along the backbone, and the other nameless shreds of stuff which had been reclaimed by the river should weigh, at a conservative guess, three pounds. After a thoughtful silence, followed by a consultation with his father, Dodger agreed to add three pounds to the recorded weight and to let that stand officially if no one contested it. It seemed eminently fair.

For the next three weeks I made frequent excuses to go to the store, and tried to look casual as I checked the board where the weights were posted. On the final day the twenty-eight and one-half pounds still stood, and I carried home the prize.

The rod was beautifully finished, but it was short and stiff, and after feeling it, I could see that it would be entirely non-functional for salmon fishing. The line was monofilament nylon – a new-fangled thing which they said was becoming standard in ocean fishing but which we had never seen before. The reel didn't have a level-wind gear, so it would hardly serve for casting a bait. And I had never seen a reel with a star drag; we always braked with the thumb against the layers of line on the reel, accepting the burns and blisters as fitting tribute to the fishes' might.

The prize made a great conversation piece, and hung on the wall for a while; then it was put away against the chance that sometime, in later life, I might see an ocean.

THE CABLE CAR

At the mouth of Yankee Fork an old rusty cable of twisted steel wires stretched across Salmon River, anchored on the near side to the base of a big cottonwood tree and on the far side to a "deadman" (a buried rock or log). Suspended from the cable on pulleys was a wooden box with two low board seats, and stretched across the river just below the cable was a rope to pull on. This cable car was a traditional adjunct to fishing at the Dam. The key to the padlock securing the car to the tree was kept at the Sunbeam Store, and could be had by asking the night before it was to be used. Crossing to the far side of the river, one then walked up to the big eddy across from The Ledge and fished from a plank resting on iron rods driven into the rock face of the cliff.

We didn't often use the cable car. However, if we had a number of people to take fishing, or if the fishing pressure had been quite high, or occasionally just for a change, we would go over and fish from The Board.

This was one of the numerous situations where one's fishing manners were put to the test. The big eddy on the far side could be fished quite adequately from The Ledge – in fact, perhaps more efficiently than from The Board – by casting some thirty yards into the far edge of the eddy where it was swinging upstream toward the cliff. If you let the bait drift in close to the cliff under The Board, it would come back toward you into the central current to be retrieved and cast again; or by pulling the line in a bit as it swung up the far side toward the cliff, one could bring it toward the center of the slowly revolving circle of water, whence it would follow down around and back toward the far side again. By making this slight adjustment each time it went around, the bait could be kept circling in the eddy indefinitely.

It was a general, unwritten assumption among the

regulars that when someone was fishing from The Board, a fisherman on The Ledge would not fish the far eddy; or, if fishing was crowded and too many people fishing, at least the man on The Ledge would keep his line out in the middle of the eddy and not let it drift in close under The Board. Occasionally, though, the eternal wheel of the eddy would twist two lines around each other. After the first thrill of mistaking it for a strike, this encounter required one protagonist to slack off line so the other could pull in the tangle and undo it. I have witnessed at least one occasion when the man on The Board reeled in the intermingled lines and, nursing resentment toward the intruding tackle, cut it off instead of untangling and releasing it. Fortunately the roar of water through the rock cut made the exchange of recriminations inaudible.

There were some anxieties involved in our use of the cable car. In the early days there was no extra rope to pull on, and pulling on the cable itself made it possible to catch ones fingers under the pulley wheel overhead. Worse yet, one year in early spring a man we knew was crossing with his wife when the water was too high, the car sagged into the water, which caught it and dragged it down enough to snap the cable. The man made it to shore but his wife did not. Thus it was always with excitement spiced with a tinge of dread that Bill and I crossed on the cable.

Once, just before reaching the far side on the car, we saw downstream and part way across the river the head of Rex, our dog, swimming against the current and being swept farther down each moment. We landed, secured the car, and raced down river, tearfully certain that Rex would never be able to make it across. When he saw us on the bank, however, he adjusted his direction and swam across instead of upstream; soon he was panting, shivering, and shaking himself in our arms. When we were through fishing and ready to start back, we debated whether to put him in the car, whence he might panic and jump out into the river and hurt himself, or to trust him to swim back across safely. The latter seemed more prudent, and so it proved to be. We gained a new respect that day for Rex's endurance and his swimming ability, if not for his good sense.

A STARTLING PIECE OF WEATHER

The four of us had taken a picnic lunch up Yankee Fork and over onto the West Fork, a small tributary to which I had never been before. Dad thought we should check out the salmon possibilities, though it seemed to me a bit small for that.

We found no salmon. After lunch we had started fishing for trout when we noticed that the sky had clouded up and was getting darker by the moment. About then a few drops of rain began to fall. We decided we'd best get back to the car, because Mom wouldn't be having much fun even if we did enjoy fishing in a downpour.

There was a brief flurry of hail, and by the time we reached the car the rain was coming down in sheets. Thunder rumbled back in the hills to the east, whence the storm was coming, and some lightning flashed around, but none of it very close.

We sat in the car for a few minutes, peering through the wall of water at the ghostly forms of trees half-visible only forty yards away. Then, as suddenly as it had come, the rain was over. We almost decided to stay a little longer, but we were all pretty wet and the thought of a fire and dry clothes was attractive, so we started home. As we got back to the main road on Yankee Fork the sun had already peeped thinly through the clouds a time or two, and it seemed as if the sky had just been teasing us and having a little fun. If it weren't for a little rivulet of water at the road's edge here and there, it would almost seem as if we had imagined the storm.

On the familiar road down Yankee Fork we had just left Jordan Creek and rounded the next bend when Dad braked abruptly to a halt – in six inches of water! Here was a place we had never seen before! Just ahead of us the road dipped down a couple of feet before rounding a point on a gentle

135

upward slope; a sheet of water lay across the road at the low spot, extending across the place where the stream channel used to be, in a lake reaching a hundred yards or so to the foot of the hill opposite. Retaining this expanse of water was a wide dam, a dike of gravel and rocks, clear across the valley from the farther side and ending, like a giant tongue, at the edge of our road. Trees, roots, and willow ends protruded randomly from the gravel. Looking across and back up the valley we could see where it all had come from: a raw, naked wound down the full length of the gulch there, as if a huge hoe had been dragged from the top of the hill down to the valley floor. Mud, flattened trees, and freshly exposed rock ledges littered the path the torrent had taken, and the vast mass of earth and debris carried by the water had been deposited in a matter of minutes athwart the stream. Looking beyond this dam, we could see that there was no stream left! Yankee Fork had been stopped in its tracks.

It took a few minutes for us to take in this awesome spectacle and to realize what had happened. The road was blocked by a couple of feet of water. How would we get home? And what would happen next?

Dad backed up a few yards and we got out of the car. We became suddenly aware of an eerie silence. Usually at this place there was a cheerful sound of water splashing over rocks, a stream perhaps thirty feet wide and averaging two to three feet deep bouncing over riffles and around boulders with sprightly abandon. Now the only sound was a faint sighing of breeze in the pines, and now and then some pebbles trickling down the new barricade. The water, opaquely brown, lay flat and motionless where brush and meadow had been a half-hour before.

As we watched in stunned fascination, we could see what was to come. The edge of this new-born lake was climbing slowly but perceptibly toward the top of the new dam, as the rather swollen stream behind us poured unsuspectingly around the bend as usual and found itself entering the lake. Within a few minutes water was seeping through the dam and then cutting away at the crest. Once it started over the top – having by now added another foot of depth across the road – it chewed and tore at the dam ever more effectively as the volume of flow through the breach increased. The level of the lake subsided, the arm of water across the road receded, and within forty-five minutes a normal downstream flow had been restored and the road was clear.

A fairly sizeable pond remained, however, as did the ragged scar down the hill and across the valley. The pond, the tongue-like deposit of rocks and gravel, and the treeless swath in the bottom of the gulch became permanent reminders of my first contact with a flash flood, cloudburst, waterspout, gully-washer, or however one's local terminology would have it. I've always felt a mixture of regret and thanks that we didn't arrive just a few minutes earlier, to be there when the action was.

BAYHORSE LAKE AND A LESSON IN BEING WILD

On days when we had all the salmon we really needed, we sometimes explored new places. Down toward Clayton we had often passed a little road and a sign which said "Kinnikinic Creek." The map told us that the road – such as it was – led to Bayhorse Lake, a very small spot on the chart a few miles off the main road. We went to see what was there.

The road followed the small creek named for a plant that the Indians used for tobacco. It went for a couple of miles and then just casually and gradually quit; the overgrown traces of it, like an old logging road, continued on visibly ahead. We parked, took our fishing gear just in case, and walked on.

Quite abruptly, after a half mile or so, we were at a small lake, maybe an acre in size. The edges were swampy, and several attempted approaches through sticky black mud under the grass convinced us that we should settle for a twenty-yard stretch on the side where a solid bank led down to the water. The character of the lake I remember as deep, dark, and mysterious. The few rising fish were all on the swampy side. Bill and I were not quite up to the casting required, but Dad caught two or three fish. They were cutthroat trout, but of a color I have never seen anywhere else: the red markings on the belly and the "slashes" on the throat, instead of the usual red-orange, were a magenta or reddish lavender, and the top of the head and back were very dark green, almost black. They were beautiful fish indeed, and we saw some more than a foot long, though the ones Dad caught were smaller. For some reason, having tried several flies and his favorite brass Colorado spinner without success, he had put on a Colorado-type spinner which was a ridiculous bright red, and it was on this alone that he caught the fish – a fact which in itself made us feel just a bit creepy about the whole place. (I later manufactured two or three red spinners from an old

Prince Albert can, but the time, much later, when we returned to Bayhorse Lake the fish showed no interest in red spinners.)

Mom explored the area about the lake and found the remains of an old brick structure which we couldn't identify – partly chimney, but not your standard fireplace left over from a burned-down house; it looked like some sort of kiln, perhaps. Mom persuaded Dad to carry home one of the double-sized bricks of which a few were mixed in with the standard kind (they were also approximately twice as heavy to carry as the usual brick).

As I was taking a detour around the swamp to try to get to another part of the lake, I saw something moving through the grass ahead of me; it looked at first like a large snake weaving back and forth and around. I hopped up onto a fallen log and, running along it, I came directly above the object and looked down on it.

The times in my life when I have seen a live weasel could be numbered on the fingers of one hand, usually a quick view as the creature has been inspecting me from the entrance of a burrow or disappearing into rocks or brush. But here I stood looking down on four weasels! The snake-like effect was an adult animal running here and there in the tall grass in circles and figures-of-eight in a seemingly confused and aimless manner, while three smaller ones – about two thirds her size – ran behind her in single file, nose to tail, so that it made a continuous moving and swerving line of weasels nearly four feet long. Once in a while the mother (my unsupported assumption took this to be maternal, not paternal, behavior) paused long enough to grab the one just behind her by the nape of the neck and drag it rapidly along for a few seconds, then dropped it and they resumed their perfect formation, for all the world like a tawny fur-covered little locomotive rushing along on silent wheels pulling three long furry tank cars on a tortuous track. At times there was a nervous chittering sound, apparently from the parent, but for the most part this amazing procession went noiselessly back and forth beneath my log, apparently oblivious of my presence.

Succumbing to the excited fascination so typical of small boys, and repressing a twinge of guilt, I slid off the log, unslung the fish landing net from around my neck, and plopped it down over the last weasel in the parade, and the others instantly disappeared. The little captive, a good eight inches long not counting the tail, at once started oozing out through a place in the mesh that wasn't over three quarters of an inch across. I quickly covered him with my hat, from which I managed to transfer him into my fish sack (a simple muslin bag). After tying the bag shut with a piece of string I waited for him to become frantic and try to tear his way out; but instead, after a few tentative trips up and down the side of the cloth, he soon curled up in a tight coil in the bottom of the bag and seemed to fall asleep. I didn't know that a weasel could purr, but this little fellow made a distinct purring sound like a kitten. All the way home, for a couple of hours, he lay hardly stirring.

He was soon ensconced in a screen cage about two by three feet and a foot deep, formerly the home of Dominick, my pet ground squirrel. He settled in nicely, casually looking and sniffing around and making no effort to get out. My knowledge of the animal's dietary needs was limited to such folk tales as a weasel raiding a chicken coop and slitting the throats of several chickens. My little friend didn't really seem up to that sort of thing, and I had no chickens to offer. Instead he eagerly accepted fat insects, and pieces of raw fish which he took from my finger. We decided not to name him for a few days until we knew him better.

He was as beautiful an animal as one could imagine. He was built just like a long flexible tube, eight inches in length and at no point much thicker than my thumb, though when hunched or fluffed up he looked three times this thick. His face was strikingly alive, and the smallness of his black eyes was made up for by the impression they gave of darting brilliance. The upper part of his body and his narrow four-inch tail were tan, and his throat and belly lemon yellow. His fur was soft and smooth, and he would curl up contentedly in my hand and fall asleep at once after eating.

Thus began a tranquil friendship – until the third day. I went to the cage as usual, and scratching on the screen brought the weasel out of the sleeping box in the corner. I reached in and handed him a juicy moth I had caught by the lamp the night before; he made short work of it. I held out my finger with a small piece of fish on it, and as usual he daintily reached up and took the fish in his mouth. This time he accidentally caught one of his needle-sharp little teeth in my skin. He jerked back against the resistance of my finger and gave a shrill snarl. Backing off to the far side of the cage, he stared at me as he devoured the fish. I offered him another piece, this time on a little flat stick. Warily he hesitated, then his head shot forward and he snatched the fish, jerking the stick in the process. Again, with a snarling sound, he retreated to the far corner of the cage to eat.

What had happened? The taste of blood, someone suggested. But he hardly pricked the finger, not nearly enough to draw blood. The only change in our act, as I could see it, was that tiny moment of my apparent resistance to his taking the food.

I still can hardly believe the instantaneous trans- formation of that animal. In the space of seconds he had changed from a cuddly pet to a totally wild and savage beast. In the three days I'd had him several people told me that you can't tame a weasel, and here was their proof. I almost never saw him motionless again; hour after hour, never resting when I was near, he moved back and forth, up and down, diagonally up the screen to the top, hop soundlessly to the floor and over to the other side and around again; he would move in a rhythmically repeated three-dimensional figure-of-eight, tirelessly and endlessly.

"Pacing" wasn't the word for it; for any other creature it would have been running, but the weasel didn't seem to run. It was a fast smooth gliding, as if he were a furry fish swimming in a tank of air. I never, of course, heard him purr again; this was replaced by the snarl at feeding time. Maybe his face hadn't changed, but the way he used it certainly had; it seemed constantly enraged and challenging.

This went on for two more days, and it became clear that any possibility of detente between me and the animal was hopeless. We held extensive family discussions as to what to do. We carefully avoided bringing outsiders into the debate; their advice even back in the brief cuddly days was to "kill the little bastard before he can escape." (Weasels do not occupy a warm spot in the mythology of most people in our day.) Ideally we should have released him back on Kinnikinic Creek, but we weren't going back there any time soon. Another source of uneasiness about releasing him was Dominick, the ground squirrel, whom I had turned loose the previous summer and who had come to visit a couple of times recently.

We compromised by carrying him in a box a few hundred yards back up on the hill across the highway, where he darted among some rocks and vanished. For a long time the sight of that empty cage kept reopening the lingering doubt in my mind: is it really impossible to tame a weasel?

THE HIGHEST ART FORM

School done for the week, after an early supper, at dusk, trotting along in delicious apprehension after Dad as he led me for the first time into Whitey's Tavern (only a little way in, as far as the pinball machine, where he let me play one game while he bantered with some men and bought a can of Prince Albert, and a Hershey bar to divide between Billy and me), I could see he was savoring this time, a ceremony strange but tantalizingly clear through my innocence, an anticipation like (as I would understand much later) touching lightly the hair of a woman you love.

Back at the car young Billy greeted us eagerly, I divided the chocolate meticulously, and Mom solemnly accepted one small square from each of us. *Thank you*, she said, and *Thank you*. In the back seat, perched on top of duffel and quilts and cooking gear, we slowly ate our candy. By the glow of the street lights Dad carefully checked tackle boxes on the floor and rods tied on top of the car. He dawdled, fiddled with his pipe, and seemed in no hurry to start.

At last our car pulled out of town onto the baseline road, gravel crunching under the tires. The rising moon cast its beam through the open window onto Mom's smooth cheek and black hair, and touched Dad's hand on the steering wheel. Billy snuggled down beside me. From across the fields came the scent of wheat harvest nearly done, an early autumn taste in the air.

With the windows closed the car soon became warm; the blankets were soft and embraced us with a subtle essence of family, a clean fragrance of dust and breath and time. My chest ached with happiness.

I awoke from time to time and peered out to check landmarks – Willow Creek Ranch, the farmhouse ghosty behind the row of poplars; the Malad Reservoir road heading in darkness through dry hills and sagebrush; the timber bridge over Wood River. Another nap and we'd passed Ketchum and already to Prairie Creek Camp, with Boulder Mountain brilliant in the moonlight. Just beyond here the beginning of Wood River looped and curved aimlessly among short willows. Billy awoke now too, and in the guise of keeping Dad from drowsiness we all sang: Old Black Joe; Let Me Call You Sweetheart; Row, Row, Row Your Boat. I tried to stay awake until Galena Summit, where the Salmon River starts as a modest trickle from a culvert under the road; but when I next was aware the moon had swept half the sky and peeped over the edge of the mountains to illuminate the dark hollows and white flourishes where Salmon River ran ponderously beside us. In another half hour we'd be there, just in time to ready our tackle and then fall into bed for maybe two hours before hitting The Ledge.

The years blend seamlessly in the archives of my mind: 1931, holding Momma's hand and watching, down in the canyon, the great rush of water spurting from the tunnel at the base of Sunbeam Dam, chinooks leaping in glorious futility and dashing their quivering bodies against the torrent, only to be thrown back into the foaming pool; 1935, the Dam breached by a channel blasted out of the mountain beside it, opening a whole new forty-mile upstream opportunity for spawning, and new vistas for fishermen with trident pitchforks or Indian style harpoons; 1937, Teddy and Billy grown in stature and competence, Ted and Bill, fishing with the grownups, learning the new technology and art of snagging salmon with hook, line, and rod.

Dad gently shook my shoulder. I nudged Bill awake and felt my way out of bed. By flashlight we found our clothes, and with rods in hand the three of us left the cabin. Mom had snuggled back into bed, murmuring good luck to us. Sometimes I worried about Mom, about us, worried that she never fished. *Oh, no*, she demurred, *I'll be fine, you go on, I just like looking after my menfolk.* I always felt the edge of something there, of something I didn't understand. Looking into Mom's eyes, above that soft smile, was sometimes like looking down a deep well. Once I flashed on the image of a butterfly pinned to a board, but the thought scared me and I swept it away.

Through the summers we competed with chinook fishermen up and down the river, getting up earlier and earlier as the season progressed to get the spot we wanted. Now the chinook run was almost finished and sensible people – unaware of the sockeyes' arrival or with no hope of catching one – had returned to work and school for the season. But we still dreaded the possibility that someone might claim the spot ahead of us, so we crept through the darkness at this daunting hour, rubbing our eyes and drawing deep tingling draughts of the crystalline air to clear our minds.

We hardly spoke during the ten-minute walk to the river; there was no need, each of us floating through his own world, I suppose, each making up his own story of what was happening. I can only speak for myself.

Dad stopped once as if to listen, not startled, not abruptly, just quit walking, turning his head from side to side. The drone of moving water came to us from down at our left, humming like a distant hive of bees – the sound, muted by a hundred yards of lodgepoles on the steep hillside, of Yankee Fork tumbling over riffles and boulders toward the main river. As we crossed the highway and dropped down a steep pitch, placing our feet cautiously on the loose gravel, a chill breeze danced up the gorge, tugging at the rods we carried, and I hunched my collar up around my ears. I fancied my tennis shoes as paws, like a panther's, feeling and adjusting to unseen rocks and dips in the path. Now the voice of the stream to our left was drowned in the insistent rumble of the river ahead where it squeezed between ragged walls of rock – or perhaps it was my heart pounding in my ears.

The moon was gone; a faint aura of pre-dawn softened the sharpness of swarming stars. As we felt our way over a flat boulder to the wet sand and grasses at the water's edge, memories rose in the muscles of the legs and each step felt as familiar as the lyrics of a favorite song. The old broken cottonwood stood to our left; a young alder leaned from the bank to our right affording a handhold for stepping over water onto scattered stones.

We hopped from rock to rock and finally onto the gravel at the foot of what had once vainly pretended to be a fish ladder. A couple of brave willows grew waist-high out of cracks in the stone, and a wild currant bush brushed our legs. Water trickled through the old tunnel which in earlier years held the entire flow of the river; here we could scoop up sucker minnows with a length of window screen for catching big trout miles down river – but not just now. We found the crude footholds and steep stairlike path that led to the uppermost part of the fish ladder.

Here, at last, was the fabled place, the queen of fishing spots, the only place on the river where the sockeyes could be consistently seen: a four by eight foot stone and concrete shelf, sheer rock face behind and a straight fifteen foot drop to the eddy below. The Ledge.

After weeks or months away, of traversing ordinary ground and mundane gravity, I always felt here a brief mystical shock, a moment of self-doubt, of readapting to the dizzying height above deep and swirling waters, to feel sure enough of my footing to ignore it and concentrate on my business. Bill leaned briefly against the wall behind us, then stepped forward. Dad put out an arm as if to gesture us back from the edge; but jerked it back, pretending to adjust his jacket. All of this reorientation was silently and quickly achieved while we once more checked our tackle by the subtly growing lucence of sky down river.

We had, the three of us jointly, invented this method and this tackle. Hundreds of people each season came to The Ledge to fish for chinooks, with bait or by snagging, but only a handful even knew of the existence of the sockeyes. These elite fish came in September and October, when the chinook run was largely played out. They wouldn't strike any known bait or lure, and were too small and too spooky to catch by the blind snagging used on the much larger chinooks. Wary as trout, sockeyes would see the line coming and sidle around ahead of it, or drop back to let it pass harmlessly in front of them.

This led us, over a couple of seasons, to a new, lighter generation of tackle. Each spring Gerrish's Hardware got a shipment of Calcutta bamboo poles from India. Alerted by telephone, we would hurry down and sort through the stack of some fifty of the rich brown, smooth-jointed poles, taking a couple of hours in the alley behind the store (while Mom did some frugal shopping or patiently waited) hefting the poles for balance, sighting down them for purity of line, and whipping them for flexibility, toughness, and soul. We debated, advised, compared. In the end, each of us swore that he had chosen the prince of rods that would out-fish all the others. We would get the necessary accessories, load up our treasure, and start the seventy-mile drive home, stopping midway for a bowl of oyster stew and crackers at the U. S. Cafe (Shorty and Slim, proprietors, were the first Chinese I ever knew) and eagerly planning the designs of the deadly-efficient rods we would make.

Perched on our rocky mezzanine we clutched the rods, each equipped with level-wind reel and braided silk line, six feet of leader, and a small treble hook. Eight inches below the hook hung a long tapered lead weight. Completing the outfit was a bit of white cloth (torn, to Mom's dismay, from the hem of a handkerchief) tied at the top of the leader for visibility when casting and maneuvering in dim light. This was the state of the art, the ultimate in sockeye tackle, the best we could imagine and devise.

We knew that each morning the sockeyes would lie at the foot of the hole beyond the great central current, where the water flattened out, the boil and froth cleared, and the rocky bottom could be seen. Their dark blue backs and some red on the sides greatly increased their visibility. Commonly from The Ledge we might count two fish, or one, or five, maybe sixty or seventy feet from us, a little platoon holding position in the current, languidly moving a few feet one way or the other with apparent casualness that was tantalizingly deceptive. We would see the same ones, singly or together, repeatedly during the day. The next morning they would have moved on up, en route to spawning in Redfish Lake, and a different group would have come in, distinguishable by sizes and colors.

As the premonition of daylight began to penetrate the blackness of the canyon floor we stood now, seriously into our work, staring at the water, squinting, heads thrust forward, straining for the first glimpse of fish.

We had already drawn straws for first shot. Dad taught us through fishing: courtesy toward other fishermen; never exceed the bag limit; take only what fish, or what bait, we could use. But we caught Dad, ever our model of rectitude, cheating as he held the three broken bunchgrass stems to insure that one of us boys drew the long straw. (Out of courtesy and respect, Bill and I never spoke of this to Dad.)

A swirl of foam was replaced for a moment by a long slick in the current and we all saw them, one bright red one and two a bit lighter and larger. They faded into the shifting reflections and shadows, then briefly appeared again. Mine was the long straw; I moved nearer the edge for freedom in casting, rod held at the ready, left thumb on the wraps of line on the spindle and the pendant-like lead clutched in my right hand.

For several minutes we watched them, discussing strategy and technique. We knew that when it was full light they would leave their exposed position and swing toward us, into deeper water and past the foot of our cliff, circle out into the white water where it rushed out of the chute, and in a few minutes would emerge on the far side and reappear where they had started. If undisturbed, that is; but we were going to disturb them.

The most promising point at which to attack was where they lay almost motionless, where the water flattened in a long sheen devoid of obstructions but moving fast. The cast must be placed with precision so that interplay of the current and the drag on the hook would combine exactly to sweep the hook in from the far side, quartering in behind and toward the fish, without lifting it too far from the bottom.

The light was growing quickly now; we could make out details of the trees on the steep hillside across from us, and the fish became more sharply, insistently visible. I measured the distance with my eye yet again, and swung the rod tip smartly outward and upward. I could barely see the splash, and my little white pennant as it dipped into the water. Two seconds later it was clear that my cast had been too short; the line was headed directly toward the fish, and I hastily retrieved it so the line or hook would not come close enough in front of them to spook them.

Feeling as if I had swung at a ball thrown low and outside, I traded places with Bill.

Bill stood for a couple of minutes, as if trying to discern the exact spot to aim for, and made his cast. It looked perfect, far enough beyond and upstream to give plenty of maneuvering room. The white flag moved into position. (You must take into account not only the depth but the refraction of light passing from water to air, the apparent depth and location of the fish). He reeled in a bit of slack, came in close to the farthest fish, and brought his rod up and backward with a mighty heave. At the same instant the fish swirled away and the hook and weight burst out of the water and shot toward us, striking the cliff just behind our ducking heads. When we looked back the three fish had vanished.

From now on it would be a waiting game. One or two of the fish might appear, resting again at the foot of the hole; but more often – maybe every fifteen or thirty minutes – one would circle in close below us, where the water was only transiently foamy, moving slowly upstream with the curl of the eddy and just deep enough so that a diffuse hint of red or blue could be glimpsed for an instant. You could drop your line out and down without an actual cast, trying to guess the depth and speed in that second or two after the dark shadow had disappeared, and take your chances, recognizing that every near miss would keep the fish more wary and likely to stay in the deeper water out of sight. Dad had one good shot, close enough to make the fish flash away; and Bill and I each took one or two unlikely tries as the prey showed less and less often and less clearly. The time was spent mostly in a tense, relentless straining of the eyes, slitted against the shifting reflections of the gradually increasing light, interspersed with shivering, rubbing hands together, and other marginally useful measures against the persistent icy breeze.

Two hours passed, and it was now full daylight. From The Ledge we could see, over the edge of the nearby rocky point and down toward Yankee Fork, just the upper corner of some rusted metal roofing with a length of stovepipe serving as chimney. As the direct sun began painting the tops of the hills gold across from us and slowly crept down the slope, we diverted more and more of our gaze from the water to that chimney.

Right on schedule: "Llew's up," Bill said, his voice raised over the din of the cataract. The thin wisp of white smoke strengthened.

"Another fifteen minutes," Dad said. Bill and I beat our arms across our chests, bounced cautiously up and down, smiled, gave one more long, intent survey of the water. The fish, offended by our moments of inattention, did not show. We secured our hooks and clambered down from The Ledge, perfume of wood smoke beckoning as we approached the box-like, paintless little house and knocked on the door.

Llew must have been expecting us; he opened the door almost instantly, and stood aside for us to enter.

"We wondered if we could come in a few minutes and get warm," Dad said.

"Yep. Coffee's ready." His voice soft, slow, precise, almost hesitant. "You catch any?"

"No", Dad said, "not yet. We got 'em riled up a little, so they're staying out of sight."

Llew's coffee-making process was a continuum: when it ran low he added more water below, more coffee above, and perked it some more. Thick and gritty in the mug, gentled with sugar and canned milk but still steaming, it was an indescribably delicious substance.

Llew had lived along these streams for fifty years as merchant, prospector, gold ore assayer, justice of the peace, caretaker for the Sunbeam Mining Company's power house, then watchman after the mines up Yankee Fork had shut down. Now, like the dam, he was a decaying relic of a bygone era, an eccentric old hermit, the butt of good natured jokes by the few locals, abandoned along with the house and dam by a corporation long extinct. And – incredible to us – he never fished; his query about our success was strictly courtesy.

151

As the enveloping warmth from the wood stove seeped into my shivering limbs, I looked around at the sparce furnishings, the grimy wallpaper, linoleum scuffed and cracked. A small bag of potatoes leaned slackly against the wall. The distinctive odors of packrats, flour, and rancid grease rose from the low cupboard. Yet there was an orderliness about the place. Llew's clothes were clean, his wispy residue of orange-white hair was brushed. A broom and dustpan stood against the wall behind the door, and his hat hung on a nail by the window. Newspapers and magazines on the floor in one corner were neatly stacked.

I felt an awe, almost a fear, of the knowledge and wisdom that must lie in the depths behind Llew's pale blue, glistening eyes. I knew that he was full of stories of the past, of history and politics and personal intrigue, but they were tightly guarded in the inner recesses of his mind. Mom, while we fished, had taken her embroidery and spent time with Llew, and over the years had unlocked many of these chambers of his memory; but to us he was politely taciturn. We kept the conversation light and shallow and granted him the respect of never asking very much.

"Thanks for the coffee," Dad said; "Guess we'll give it another try." Bill and I added our thanks. We picked up our rods from where they leaned against the house and walked back toward The Ledge.

Now, in the sunshine, the dam itself stood alone, exiled and embarrassed, ignored by the river. The quaintly formless and pitted concrete face sloped down into a stagnant green pool, its right flank mocked by a skimpy skeleton of decayed timbers and rusted metal powerhouse remnants that had survived the scrap collectors. The old tunnel, perhaps ten feet across and fifty feet long, cradled a trickle among the stones and was cool and dim in the hottest weather; Lew kept a screen cage deep inside for butter and meat.

We resumed our vigil, catching sometimes a fleeting glimpse of dark beneath the froth, or of dull red against the green, disappearing as it passed below us; rarely one showed in the edge of the heavy current. Seeing was a constant effort, squinting against the glare of sun bouncing off the water, peering between the shifting lines of white and through transient slicks or swirls free of bubbles.

Neck aching, lids burning with the effort and the reflected rays, I occasionally dared look away, to take in the details of our surroundings. Across the river, below a fringe of Indian paintbrush and dry grass, a steep shale slope plunged down abruptly to the edge of the big eddy. Dancing among stones at the water's edge was a blue-gray bird, a water ouzel or "dipper", bobbing up and down for a few seconds on a rock, jumping to another rock, then walking into the water, walking along the bottom of the shallows completely submerged for a few seconds, then regaining his perch on the rock.

Twice Dad made a cast, but each time the quarry was out of sight seconds before the line arrived at the intended spot, and the hopeful upward sweep of the rod was in vain. Once I saw one moving through the lower end of the hole, but my hasty cast was hardly close to where the fish disappeared.

The midday heat had relieved us of our shirts and pressed down onto the rock. The sun passed its meridian.

Dad asked, "Would you like to go down the river and try for trout?" Bill and I looked at each other.

"We know they're still in here," I said.

"And remember that time you caught one in the afternoon?" asked Bill. Dad smiled, and didn't bother to reply. We continued our intense surveillance.

We didn't know then that fifty years earlier the fish had passed this spot by the thousands to spawn in Alturas, Pettit, Redfish, and Stanley Lakes. (In 1881 a prospector took 2,600 pounds of fresh sockeyes from Alturas Lake to sell to miners.)

Nor did we know that just fifty years later only two sockeyes would return during the entire summer-fall season, an ancient race headed for extinction; nor that The Ledge would be gone, pried loose by rain seeping into cracks and freezing, the whole face of the cliff ignominiously collapsed into the river; nor that this was the last time we would all enact this ceremony together.

But on this day, this day in the exact center of time, the world was whole and good. The mountain clutched the river to steady it as it roared through the cut to our right; the water twirled in two eddies before us like ballroom dancers, then flattened and swept away with a flourish toward the Pacific, nine hundred miles away around the next bend. The treetops glowed gold with the sinking sun. The ouzel was gone, a crisp breeze from down the canyon licked our faces, our water jar was empty, and we stood straining for a last morsel, a last glimpse of the phantoms that faded in and out of shadows, and out of our lives.